Watford Miniature Railway

Steaming to Sixty

Dr Rudi Newman

First published in 2019

ISBN 978-1-5272-3590-8

Published by Southern Miniature Railways Ltd.

For more by the author, enquire at any good book store.

Cover images courtesy of S. Mulligan, R. Newman, C. O'Mahoney and D. Robinson.

Contents

With thanks to all who have assisted with this project, and everyone who has worked on the railway bringing joy to countless people.

Introduction

Railways have always been important to Britain. Having countless impacts, alongside their commercial and industrial involvement they have also been a great cultural influence. Whether little children wanting to grow up to be train drivers, the romance of lovers on a platform in black-and-white films, or simply the enthusiasm of people towards steam – as demonstrated by the *Flying Scotsman* – they hold an important place in the public psyche.

2019 marks the 60th anniversary of one particular railway. Not built for heavy freight or rapid transit, instead it is one of many railways built in miniature, simply for the pleasure of travelling by train. But the Watford Miniature Railway, the 'Cassiobury Park Line', is more than just a toy. Enjoyed by generation after generation, what is particularly delightful is how, sixty years after first being built, it continues to perform its original task: having passengers leave a little bit happier than when they arrived.

This book is the result of much work and collaboration, telling the story of the railway in two ways. It opens with a traditional overview – how the site and line came to be, the changes it encountered and the engines that graced its rails. The narrative then turns, however, to those who were there and helped make it happen. Presented in their own words, it reveals both the events and actions, but also the dedication and enthusiasm behind their efforts.

The history of this line is one of serving the community, but it also shows how much it is appreciated.

Enjoy the journey.

The first Railway through Cassiobury – Almost!

When Cornishman Richard Trevithick invented the steam railway locomotive, undertaking a series of experiments in the early 1800s, he could scarcely have imagined the consequences of his actions. Triggering industrial and technological expansion on a scale scarcely seen in human history, railway construction exploded into the international transport networks we know today, impacting on every part of life and helping shape the modern world.

Steam railways as a technology were well established by the 1830s, most famously the Liverpool & Manchester Railway with Robert Stephenson's iconic locomotive *Rocket*. Prior to the great Victorian

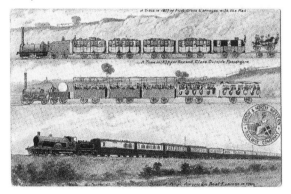

'railway manias' that created Britain's rail network though, passenger railways were few in number, many people being wary of this new and untested method of transportation. The construction of the 112-mile London & Birmingham Railway (L&BR), opened in

Rail development 1837-1904 (Author's Collection).

1838, was a watershed – the first cross-country main line 'trunk' railway, today part of the West Coast Main Line. Designed by Robert Stephenson, it intended to promote trade and travel between the two cities, but was not without opposition, as the railway's surveyors found when they visited Watford in 1834:

5

'The Farmers, naturally indignant, ordered these intruders from their fields. The engineers, for such they were, took but little notice. The farmers proceeded to threats.

The ringleader of the invaders produced a red book, folded in an oblong form, from the voluminous pocket of his velveteen jacket, and offered it to the irate farmer as a sedative, informing him that it was the Act of Parliament by authority of which he was acting...

One thing alone remained for them [the farmers] to do...they would shoot the intruders!

But the latter calmly replied that that was no business of theirs, and the farmers did not draw trigger.'

WATFORD, CANAL BRIDGE, CASSIOBURY PARK   70394

The Canal, Cassiobury (Author's Collection).

People were frightened of the effects that the railway could have – on land values, farming (scaring cows and horses), and on the scenery of the countryside itself. In a time before 'compulsory purchase', the L&BR had to privately purchase every piece of land needed. Where landowners refused they would have to either pay large amounts of compensation or divert the route of the railway – something that happened several times during the design stages. Meetings were held in public houses across affected parts of Hertfordshire, influential landowners in particular wanting to protect their estates. One such meeting, held in Watford, was attended by two particularly important individuals.

Owner of the Cassiobury Estate, George Capel-Coningsby, 5th Earl of Essex, was decidedly against the 'iron horse', as was John Villiers, 3rd Earl of Clarendon, owner of the neighbouring Grove Estate. The L&BR wanted the flattest route, so planned to follow the Grand Junction Canal (later merged into the Grand Union). This had been built across Essex's land – although with substantial compensation paid. The railway would pass south of Watford in a gentle curve, but Essex and Clarendon were having none of that.

Cassiobury House, from a period postcard (Author's Collection).

Belonging to the Capel family since 1627, in the 17th Century Cassiobury House had been extensively remodelled from its Tudor origins. It was lavishly decorated in the latest fashion, later gaining a Gothic exterior. The estate itself comprised a private 693-acre park divided in two by the river, with lodge buildings and extensive landscaping. When built across the grounds, even the canal – then the equivalent of today's motorways – was forced to be widened and landscaped to better suit its picturesque surroundings. Rebuilding of the House was finally completed by 1805 and the railway, with its smoke and machinery, was thought too unsightly to be allowed – a common view amongst major landowners of the time.

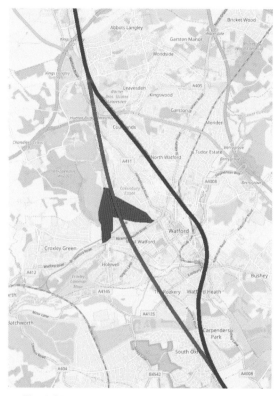

The L&BR as designed in red and built in blue (based on OpenStreetMap Project data).

Blocking any route over the estate, the L&BR was forced to divert the railway to the north. Instead of the easily-built gentle curve, the new line required construction of the Watford Tunnel and several viaducts – all costly and previously unnecessary. Still visible on maps today, the deviation ultimately led to the modern position of Watford Junction and its connection to the St Albans Abbey branch line, the creation of Bushey station (built in 1841) and the subsequent growth of commuter suburbs around them. None of these would have occurred if the Cassiobury Estate had been built on: such was the power of Essex, Clarendon and the period's landowners.

George Capel-Coningsby's son, the 7th Earl of Essex, continued to live at Cassiobury, ironically marrying the heiress of the American

Grant Locomotive Works, but after his death the House and estate were put up for sale. Much of the land was sold for housing development around the nearby Watford Underground Station, opened in 1925, while the unsold House was demolished in 1927. The neighbouring Grove House remains, now a hotel but ironically at one point belonging to British Rail!

The former L&BR at Bushey c.1910 (Author's Collection).

While much of the Cassiobury Estate was built on, other parts becoming the West Herts Golf Course, in 1909 Watford Borough Council purchased 184 acres of the former estate. Some was developed, but most was designated a public park. Another railway incursion threatened in 1929 with a proposed extension of the Metropolitan Railway to the centre of Watford High Street. One of the two intended routes crossed the Park, but ultimately neither was constructed. The Park was extended in 1930 and today comprises 190 acres – a Grade II listed nature reserve of historical, ecological and scientific interest.

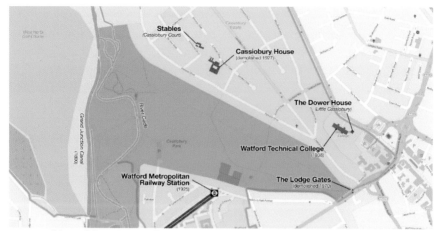

Map of Cassiobury Park (based on OpenStreetMap Project data).

While not done for these intentions, in protecting his estate from the L&BR the 5th Earl of Essex created the seeds of the Cassiobury Park we know today. Now recognised as one of the finest public parks in the country, perhaps he was right after all…

The former estate Lodge Gates (Author's Collection).

Railways in Miniature

In the early years of railway development there were a variety of gauges of track, but by the 1840s the most widely-used became a standard still used across the world today: 4 foot 8½ inches. While predominant, this 'standard gauge' was not viable for lines with limited space though, such as through mountainous terrain or in heavy industry. Quarries in particular opted for a smaller 'narrow gauge', but it was initially thought impossible to build a useable steam engine this small. However, the successful introduction in 1863 of steam power on the 1 foot 11½-inch Ffestiniog Railway, Wales, heralded worldwide application of ever-smaller railways.

Ffestiniog Railway locomotive Princess (Author).

In the 1870s a 15-inch gauge light railway design for use on large estates was created by Arthur Heywood, suggesting this was the smallest practical size possible, dubbed 'minimum gauge'. While the smallest genuine railway (as opposed to model or scale), enthusiasts, however, had begun constructing their own considerably smaller rideable engines and track. Commonly built to 10¼-inch gauge as on the Watford Miniature Railway (and after World War Two increasingly to 7¼-inch), unlike Heywood's designs – which rapidly succumbed to rising numbers of lorries – these little trains were privately built purely for the enjoyment of operating their own steam locomotives. Of particular note, in 1890 a private line was built at Pitmaston Manor, Moor Green (Birmingham) by Sir John

11

Holder – its success cementing the standard of 10¼-inch gauge and the practicality of miniature railways as a whole. Seeing a market, Northampton model-making firm Bassett-Lowke began developing castings and completed engines in 1910, becoming one of the biggest names in model engineering and helping foster a new type of travel: miniature or 'park' railways. Operating solely for entertainment rather than transporting goods or getting to any destination, numerous developed in the Edwardian Era and became popular fixtures of many seaside resorts.

The Llewelyn Miniature Railway, Southport, 1911 (Author's Collection).

Although diminishing somewhat over the two World Wars there was a resurgence in such lines in the 1960-70s, quite likely encouraged by the well-publicised 1951 Festival of Britain 'Far Tottering & Oyster Creek Railway' based on the *Punch* magazine cartoons by Roland Emmett.

What may be less known though is that Watford was at the forefront of this miniature railway development.

George Flooks

Yorkshireman George Flooks, aided by business partner Fred Smithies, established a model engineering firm in Leavesden Road, Watford around 1900. Developing their own design of miniature steam boiler, they constructed a 10¼-inch gauge steam engine called *Nipper* and in 1904 opened a 200-yard miniature railway at Woodside Pleasure Grounds, Bricket Wood. Part of a funfair growing in popularity (the connecting St Albans Abbey branch line gaining lengthened platforms for excursion specials), this was the first commercial miniature railways in Britain – open to the public rather than just for private use. Sadly it closed after a single season, purportedly as a derailment broke Smithies leg. With the engineering firm dissolved, the railway equipment was sold to Wenman Bassett-Lowke (founder of the then-fledgling model company).

Nipper at Bricket Wood, from a period postcard (M. Webb).

Used in Northampton, this was a trial prior to the company commencing miniature locomotive production from 1905. Nipper passed through various owners including Captain Vivian Hewitt of Anglesey and Sir William McAlpine, and still survives today.

One of Flooks' later 12-inch gauge locomotives at Bricket Wood, from a period postcard (M. Webb).

In 1905 George Flooks built a completely new second railway at Bricket Wood to 12-inch gauge for added stability. The railway moved to The Paddock in Northwood after World War One, closing in the mid-1920s. He continued building engines, his last completed in 1935. Named *Prince Edward* (first steamed on the day he was born, 9th October 1935), it was later purchased in 1944 by the Grand Union Canal Company when establishing the Ruislip Lido Railway – the line being gauged to the engine. Used there until the 1960s it worked various lines across the country and today survives privately owned in Lincolnshire.

Henry Greenly

While Flooks may be lesser-known, another Watford resident remains famed in the world of miniature engineering. Born in 1876, Henry Greenly rose to become an engineer working for the Metropolitan Railway at Neasden. When 24 years old he won multiple competitions organised by *Model Engineering* magazine;

details of one (a 4-4-0 locomotive) became not only his first published design but also the basis for Flooks' *Nipper*. Smithies even contacted Greenly asking for his input on redesigning some elements.

Now working for *Model Engineering*, in 1904 he, his wife and daughter moved from London to Birch Grove, Watford. Greenly subsequently left *Model Engineering*, becoming a freelance designer and publishing numerous books alongside his own magazine. In 1914, however, he left Watford and moved to Farnborough to work at the Royal Aircraft Factory during World War One. Having met Wenman Bassett-Lowke in 1900, Greenly increasingly acted as consultant for the model company, being involved in the establishment of the miniature railways subsidiary that had purchased Flooks' original 10¼-inch railway. His reputation continued to grow and he received several contracts to act as engineer for miniature railways under construction. One, the Ravenglass & Eskdale Railway, was a narrow-gauge line rebuilt to 15-inch gauge by Bassett-Lowke for which he designed locomotive *River Esk*.

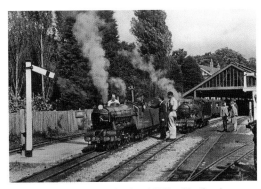

Hythe Station in the 1950s (Author's Collection).

In 1924 he began designing two 15-inch 4-6-2 'pacifics' for Count Louis Zborowski and Captain John Howey. Although Zborowski died shortly afterwards in a racing accident, Howey continued with the project – a complete main line railway in miniature. Greenly recommended a 15-inch gauge and location, between New Romney and Hythe, Kent, and in 1925 became the railway's chief engineer. He designed virtually the entire railway, from locomotives and track to signal boxes, and extended the line to Dungeness in 1928 – a total length of 13½ miles. Now preserved, over its life the Romney, Hythe & Dymchurch Railway (RH&DR) progressed from essentially a 'toy' to a recognised public main line, albeit only one third the usual size. During World War Two it even boasted a functioning armoured train!

Greenly left the RH&DR in 1929 and founded a short-lived model engineering firm in the late 1930s. He continued his writing and model designing alongside other work throughout World War Two, until his death in 1947. Today this one-time Watford resident is remembered as one of the foremost model engineers of all time.

RH&DR Typhoon and LNER Flying Scotsman - same class, different scale!
(Author's Collection)

Hertfordshire has many other links to miniature railways, from semi-professional engineers to enthusiast-led portable lines. It even aided narrow gauge preservation when plans for a rail attraction at Garston Park, Watford, instead led to Bedfordshire's Leighton Buzzard Narrow Gauge Railway being saved. But it is interesting that the region was also directly involved with two key individuals that helped create the modern-day 'miniature railway'.

A Brief History of the WMR

The WMR owes its origins to two men: Charlie Reed and George Webb. Working for Scammells of Watford during World War Two, they first met on the gun-tractor production line and quickly became firm friends. After the War Charlie began to develop an independent engineering firm based at Bushey Heath, and with it becoming a successful business he decided to leave Scammells. The work was extremely varied, ranging from servicing the local bank manager's American car to maintaining rides at Battersea Funfair (near the Festival of

Charlie Reed and George Webb (C. Reed courtesy of J. Price Collection & M. Webb).

Britain's miniature 'Far Tottering and Oyster Creek Railway'). Meanwhile George was called out of reserve occupation in 1947 to finish his National Service. On completion he joined Charlie at his Bushey Heath Firm, in particular helping with welding and reconditioning old engines – notably from the Ford Model Y car (also known as the 'Ford Eight').

The Portable Railway

Charlie had already considered the idea of creating a miniature railway while still at Scammells, some old vehicle channel section being collected as impromptu rail (later used in the sidings at Cassiobury until well into the late 1970s). Little was attempted, however, until around 1949 when Charlie was given a set of miniature locomotive wheel castings to settle a debt. This presented the final necessary impetus and a small portable line was built as a side venture from the engineering firm, for use at fetes and parties.

The original Jimpy on the portable line (M. Webb).

With the wheel castings married to an ex-War Department engine, a 10¼-inch gauge steam outline locomotive was built called *Jimpy* (joined by some sit-astride coaches), while 13-foot stretches of horseshoe iron bar from the local blacksmiths were welded into an oval of track. Completed in 1950 and travelling between events for several years, it proved very popular. On one early outing they were preparing to dismantle the track after providing rides for children at a party, only for the parents to ask for a turn! The first season alone saw ten outings, Charlie and George increasingly being assisted by a local girl, Cathy, who became the main driver. For ease the line developed into a straight out-and-back format, *Jimpy* gaining a reverse gear for the task, but with the effort needed to continually move the temporary track Charlie began to contemplate a permanent site.

The First Permanent Lines

Jimpy at the Rickmansworth Aquadrome, 1953 (M Webb).

Having worked with various showmen repairing machinery, contacts led to a prospective site at a Blackpool fairground around 1952-3. Track was laid, but in the wind sand from the beach blew into the axle boxes and, mixing with the lubricating oil, formed a paste that began to wear the bearings down. Before the end of the season Charlie had pulled out, having found another potential site. The temporary track was laid at Rickmansworth Aquadrome for the 1953 Coronation, complete with a tunnel repurposed from a canvas road-menders' shelter, and this location seem well-suited. The Aquadrome at the time was privately owned though and an agreement could not be met, so the search continued – sites being considered in a Dorset zoo (track actually being laid but never opened) and even a Southend pub beer garden.

By this time Charlie's business had closed, Charlie and George parting company. They briefly found each other later working for the same company, spending time discussing miniature railways, before Charlie changed jobs again. Prior to their reunion, Charlie had contacted the Stoke Newington Council, London, regarding Clissold Park. Permission was granted (likely around 1954-5) and a permanent line was constructed in the Park along Church Street by the paddling pools – a simple out-and-back layout. *Jimpy* was rebuilt for additional power (ultimately twice), new coaches assembled from angle-iron and the line opened around 1956-7. Although well received, Charlie still looked for

The Clissold Park Railway (C. Reed courtesy of J. Price Collection).

alternate sites, ultimately selling the Clissold line in the early 1960s

Clissold Park, 2018. Note the former track bed to the left (D. Dowling).

after the WMR had been established, as running the two sites together was not viable. This did not go to plan, however, as *Jimpy* (included in the sale) broke a wheel and the new owners defaulted on payment. By the time Charlie returned to Clissold Park she had been lost to arson, and the railway was subsequently dismantled around 1962-3.

Today traces of the track beds still remain.

Cassiobury Park

Despite having established a permanent line at Clissold Park, Charlie was still searching for locations. In 1957 a second locomotive was built (based on an 08 shunter) and, when the Hunstanton Pier miniature railway was redeveloped in 1958, he purchased coaches, track and the steam engine *Maid Marion*. In

Maid Marion on the original WMR track (C. Reed courtesy of J. Price Collection).

October 1958 he approached the Parks & Recreation Grounds Committee of Watford Borough Council. Charlie's plan was to establish a 350 yard-long line in Cassiobury Park, Watford, near Gade Avenue (today the Park's car park entrance), intending it to be close to the paddling pool. In return for Council-funded accommodation for equipment, the Borough engineer estimating a cost of £70-100 for the shed/s needed, Charlie proposed a 6d fare with the income to be divided 40% for the Council and 60% for himself. Discussed by the Committee on 20th October 1958, they withheld a decision until they could inspect the revenue from other such council-supported miniature railways.

Maid Marion viewed across the river at Cassiobury Park c.1959-62 (C. Reed courtesy of J. Price Collection).

Two local authorities provided positive financial details, but by December the question of permission was still delayed as a site within the Park had yet to be agreed upon. The Parks Superintendent investigated several locations, but ultimately Charlie and the Committee agreed on a site by the pool on 'the triangular piece of land bordered by the River Gade'. This was finalised by 23rd February 1959, with £100 reserved from the upcoming Park budget and the Borough Engineer to design a shed screened with shrubs. The line was built as 150 yards of track running along the river in an L shape making a triangle with path. The track itself was laid with the assistance of George Storrow, a British Railways engine cleaner at Watford who met Charlie through driver colleague Ken Morris, both occasionally driving *Jimpy* at Clissold. Rolling along on a carriage bogie to test the track, the first attempt led to a few scrapes and bruises! A three-year license was granted on 6th Apr 1959 and, opening shortly after, the Watford Miniature Railway was born.

Charlie Reed and Maid Marion at the original WMR station (C. Reed courtesy of J. Price Collection).

The Charlie Reed Years: 1959 – 1968

Initially only *Maid Marion* operated at Cassiobury, but by 1960 the 08 diesel moved from Clissold to assist. Once the line was established the timetable of operation developed – April to September, weekends and school holidays. Various people joined the railway as staff, notably Eric Sibil, a friend of Charlie's acting as driver, and Mrs Amy Reed as ticket lady. Children often gathered simply to watch the trains and several would later help out, such as the teenage Rainbow brothers. The Council provided tickets and took a share of takings, but significantly this was from the overall gross total, not from profits alone. Fortunately the line was very successful: the 1960 season saw passenger numbers increase 50% with over 15,000 tickets sold that year. Buoyed by this, in October that year the Parks Superintendent suggested to the Parks & Recreation Grounds Committee the idea of improving the line and boosting amenities at this end of the Park.

The initial WMR route c.1958-62 (C. Reed courtesy of J. Price Collection).

By January 1961 the Council were sufficiently enthusiastic that the upcoming license renewal was arranged for seven years instead of three (the original expiring on 30th September 1961). Furthermore, the Parks Superintendent submitted a plan for a new railway layout with a larger station by the paddling pool and the line running through a tunnel of laburnums, passing over two bridges across a water channel and winding through a model village complete with nursery figures. Estimated at £750, this plan was to be submitted to Charlie and the costs reserved from the 1961-2 and 1962-3 budgets (£450 and £300 respectively). Charlie agreed to the new layout, having already considered an extension and acquired additional track, but emphasised that he could not financially contribute to the

proposals. Instead, he suggested any income exceeding £450 per season be divided equally between the Council and himself (under this amount remaining at 60%-40% as before).

The resulting discussions caused delays, so the previous three-year license was extended to Easter

The 08 Diesel new at Cassiobury (C. Reed courtesy of J. Price Collection).

1962 rather than deal with the new seven-year proposal alongside the ongoing layout talks. But when put to Charlie in September 1961 he was very reticent about the seven year duration, instead requesting a monthly license. Such a major change disconcerted the Parks Committee, who wanted assurances that the railway would still operate – particularly as they were about to fund a £750 improvement scheme and felt that the longer lease offered Charlie extra security. Charlie's actions, however, were much more logical than they may first seem, particularly as he simultaneously requested a second shed for rolling stock. From the opening of the line many of the coaches were stored outside chained to the tracks, and he had repeatedly suffered from vandalism often costing around

£20-25 each time in repairs. As Charlie explained back in 1959 to the local press, 'expenses like these could cripple the railway' (then still considered 'experimental'), warning that repair costs could block any extension plans – plainly long under consideration by 1961. This news report, conversely, demonstrates that even after barely four months of operation the WMR had already had a significant impact on Watford: the 'Cassiobury Park Special' attracting children 'thrilled to a miniature train ride in their thousands'. By October 1961 Charlie and the Parks Committee had come to an agreement, with the seven-year lease to be signed as long as the Council 'provided certain improvements' (such as the new stock shed).

Maid Marion on her last day in service, 1966 (M. Webb).

Unfortunately, with one problem resolved another surfaced – water. The railway's river-side site was susceptible to flooding, on occasions stopping the railway from running at all. With the Council's extension plans, Charlie asked if the track could be raised by one foot, to cost the Council approximately £200. While the Thames Conservancy Board dredged the river, discussions were made concerning alternate sites for the line. These were swiftly discounted on safety grounds though; a riverbank suggestion being considered dangerous for other Park users plus the risk in case of accident of passengers being 'thrown into the river'. With the only solution being to physically raise the land, a sewerage scheme at Nascot Wood was mentioned as a possible source of soil. By January 1962 it was plain that there would not be enough soil from this, so it was decided that the extension plans be scaled back to allow for further material costs within the aforementioned £750. In February 1962 Charlie agreed to sign a new lease, but ultimately the land was never raised and the envisioned model village line never built. Even today the line occasionally floods, with dramatic effect…

Trevithick marooned by floodwater, c.1990s (J. Price).

In spite of the failure of the Council's grand plan, the railway would still see changes. A second shed for rolling stock was constructed as requested and by 1963, with the help of the Rainbow brothers, the route had been extended to a continuous circuit complete with a dedicated station. Operation of the railway on this new route continued for several years, the 08 diesel increasingly taking the strain as *Maid Marion* was worn out. Charlie was now working for Gleasons engineering, and in 1967 the firm relocated to Plymouth. Not long for retirement, he decided to follow the firm and pass the railway (minus *Maid Marion*) on to a new owner. Charlie contacted his old friend to offer him the line, and in 1968 George Webb became the new operator of the WMR.

The 08 diesel at the spur station, 1966 (M. Webb).

The George Webb Years: 1968 – 1979

The first task awaiting George on taking over the line stemmed from the flooding issues that had ended the Council's plans. With the railway's site suffering from a high water table, the track's wooden sleepers had a shorter working life with regular re-laying necessary. This was worsened in 1969 when the Water Board undertook a major drainage operation, building a new sewer across the Park and under the river. Much of the track circuit by the river had to be temporarily removed, the line running a reduced service, and some rails were damaged when the Board's digger ran over them!

Running amid the diggers (M. Webb).

Balancing the railway with full-time employment, George was supported by numerous volunteers who were vital in helping keep the line running, particularly with re-sleepering work and ongoing spates of vandalism. Of particular note were his son Malcolm, who helped in the holidays between studies, and Jeff Price. Joining the Watford Miniature Railway as a teenager in 1969 Jeff was initially involved in track-work, his first task assisting with altering the overly-tight curve by the sheds and later undertaking track laying (notably after the Water Board's digger...). The line still depended on the 08 diesel, although a miniature 'Terrier' steam engine did operate occasionally from the mid 1970's (albeit only on the track alongside the path), and Jeff soon became a senior driver and ultimately George's primary assistant.

George Webb and the 'Terrier' c.1976 with the old pool in the background (M. Webb).

In 1970 the Council initiated wider discussions on Park amenity development. A railway extension was briefly considered, as was a Council proposal in 1974 to entirely relocate the railway. Under this plan it would have been rebuilt between the river and canal (complete with tunnels and landscaping) so the former railway site could become a boating lake. With local fears of the Park being turned into a 'theme park', the *Friends of Cassiobury Park* was formed in 1973 as a result of these Council discussions, protecting the character of the Park.

In part linked with these wider developments, by the early 1970s the Council's stance on Park maintenance had changed. Gone were the days of a manicured vista akin to stately house gardens, instead parks looking to encourage nature and be more 'wild'. The WMR site had originally been devoid of vegetation, simply a patch of regularly-mown grass, but trees began to be encouraged (such as the 1973 government 'plant a tree' campaign) and the centre of the circuit was left to nature. Visitors today would surely assume, quite

29

incorrectly, that the trees are older than the trains... A problem increasingly arose though. The early out-and-back line had been fenced off, but this was removed when the circuit was developed. New fencing required Council permission, so the line had to operate with no barrier from pedestrians – forcing

Taking the curve away from the path, c.1970s. Note the unmown grass (M. Webb).

drivers to continually look backwards to ensure passenger safety as much as forwards for a clear track. This situation remained until the line was fenced off in stages from 1986. As Jeff later recalled: 'The old lady with her dog off the lead was the nightmare scenario for the driver: watch the dog or the owner!'

The difficulty of fenceless operation (M. Webb).

With the track issues resolved and a wider group of individuals to help with trains and maintenance, the railway continued operations throughout the 1970s. George retired in 1979 and decided to move to the Isle of Wight. The railway was advertised for 18 months in *Model Engineer* magazine, but George resisted a number of offers to sell the railway off-site during this period. An Easter time visit to Cassiobury Park, however, resulted in an agreement. Having left the railway in 1974 to begin a career in engineering, long-standing WMR supporter Jeff Price became the line's third owner, commencing new operations on 1st May 1979.

The Jeff Price Years: 1979 – 2017

Taking over the railway with three coaches and the 08 diesel, Jeff immediately set about long-term developments. Once a new license was issued for 1980 (Jeff previously operating temporarily with no formal license), these began with relaying the entire track – replacing the wooden sleepers with steel ones so improving longevity in damp ground. New supplies greatly aided this; a rail bender Jim Crow found at Neasden was particularly welcome as previously rails could only be bent by using the fork of a suitable tree and plenty of heaving on the free end…! Vandalism had decreased by this time, but 1980 saw a brief resurgence – fortunately causing little damage.

With improved track Jeff turned to expanding the locomotive fleet. In 1980 he acquired additional coaches and a new petrol engine of the 'Meteor' class in 1981. These were followed in 1983 by a major development for the WMR: reintroduction of steam services with the purchase of Atlantic 4442. Additional rolling stock followed, the fleet growing to seven by 1985 including two steam engines (Atlantic 4442 and *Chiltern Shuttle*). With the sights and sounds of steam reinvigorating the line, further engines appeared until for the first time a full steam-only service was made possible, by the mid-1990s having four steam engines available on top of the diesel fleet.

Meteor V on the pathside stretch (G. Fairweather).

Chiltern Shuttle in the first spur station (D. Horton).

Alongside seven-day-a-week running in the summer months – carrying around 45,000 passengers annually – a new portable line was also operated in the 1980s. Going back to its roots, the railway could again offer a travelling service for fetes and functions, such as the annual Watford carnival at the upper end of Cassiobury Park. Whenever travelling further afield, it often helped promote the railway and Watford as a whole. Fares had to cover rising fuel prices though, the erstwhile 6d fare changing in stages from 15p in 1983 to 50p in 1993. There were also other challenges: Water Board work in 1985 disrupted operation, track being moved and damaged again as had occurred under George Webb back in 1969. However, with the railway now settled into regular operation it was aided by many volunteers and supporters – notably several teenagers who went on to engineering careers just as Jeff himself had undertaken.

Atlantic 4442 working the portable railway, St Albans 1983 (J. Price).

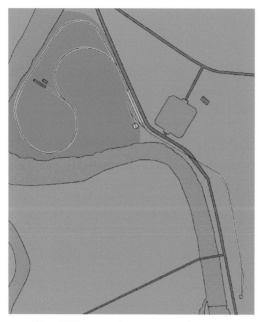

The 1981 extension proposal (Author).

These were not the only changes planned though. Jeff began to explore the potential for a substantial modification of the line's route, to be operated under a longer license. Various plans were explored but proved unfeasible both in gaining permission and in operation limitations. The most promising, which even went as far as being submitted in an official planning application in 1981, would have seen the station area expanded with loop and sidings, sheds relocated, a modified circuit, and most significantly an extension along the river heading south towards the Park's lower car park with a second station area. One other idea would have seen the line cross the river (by a bridge near the current level crossing), run across the land by the river's west bank to the bridge over the canal at Rousebarn Lane, then pass along the bottom edge of the golf course, and up through Whippendell Woods to the Grove Mill Lane car park – a considerable run. This was, however, discounted very early on as

Jeff Price and Atlantic 4442 on the portable line at the 1983 Watford Carnival (J. Price).

wishful thinking! Jeff equally intended to create a small museum display, the line by the 1990s having gained various historic miniature locomotives either in operation or storage.

Meteor V running a service in the 1980s (G. Fairweather).

Although these plans came to naught, the WMR would nonetheless gain its extension. The circuit station had originally been close to the children's paddling pool – pivotal in selecting the railway's site in the first place. Built in 1933, this was located by the River Gade and had always been very popular. But in winter 1985 it was closed and a new pool complex was built nearby – potential passengers consequently congregating further away from the spur station. The following year the old pool was filled in, its drains helping with the area's high water table. Now vacant land, a circle of portable track was briefly laid there (helped by a visiting 'Terrier' steam engine) as a service for the September 1986 'Watford Community Fun Day' – a Council-led event supporting disadvantaged children.

When the Council's new pool discussions first began in 1979, and with this large space to become available, Jeff proposed a major railway extension. Various options were considered as outlined, even changing location outright, but the format ultimately agreed upon would include a brand new station on this vacant plot leading to a lengthened route on the line's current site, created by installing a linking track across the centre of the circuit so making a loop. Not only would this give a longer run with greater passenger capacity, but it made operations simpler for the driver – no longer needing to worry as much about straying passengers or pedestrians when reversing into the spur station. Most importantly, it would transform what some considered to be virtually a 'mechanical child minder' into a more interesting and authentic railway experience.

Four in steam: the fleet in 1994 (D. Robinson).

Initial intentions for the extension stretch included a new two-platform station, sections of double-track operation when leaving the station and even a semi-automated twin-track level crossing, but these were ultimately scaled back. A reminder of the proposal remains though in the wider track bed on the station side of the level crossing. Instead, a separate 7¼-inch gauge out-and-back line was installed in this area, which ironically never saw a single train.

The wider track bed by the level crossing, with 7¼-inch track in situ, 2000
(C. O'Mahoney).

Although simplified, the project was still not without difficulties. There was some opposition to the scheme, objecting to the line crossing the path plus concerns the expansion would commercialise the Park, but these proved unfounded. The crossing was originally un-gated while safety barriers were constructed but there were problems with parents standing in front of trains to take photographs, resulting in the rapid installation of the current gates in January 1988. Similarly there were lengthy Council discussions on fencing, from its installation to its colour... More significant though, an error in the planning application site drawing placed part

Trevithick on the modified circuit c.1991-4 (J. Price).

of the new station some yards outside of the leased ground. This resulted in the need for a temporary terminus until a further planning application could be submitted. With the lease area extended, the track could then be slewed over to a new turntable and platform. Fortunately the Council laid their new connecting path in the correct location, simplifying the task. In the meantime a temporary turntable was fitted and the station opened for service by Christmas 1987. This was ultimately replaced by the new station, a few yards to the east of the former.

Over the 1990s and with the new station, various special services were introduced in support of local charities such as for bonfire night and Santa. In October 1992 the WMR even hosted a more unusual event: a reception congratulating Jeff on his recent wedding. The railway's extension, coupled to increasing park footfall and the ability to run two-train services led to significantly increasing passenger numbers, in turn leading to a need for more coaches and engines (such as steam engine *Trevithick* in 1990). The closure of the miniature railway at Suffolk Wildlife Park, Kessingland, provided much material: coaches, diesels (*Conway Castle* and *Nikki Louise*, to become the mainstay of the WMR's later motive power) and additional track arriving in 1992. This track would be used in July 1994 for a slight expansion of the station and route, creating the longest track layout in the line's history.

Nikki Louise and Conway Castle arriving at Cassiobury (J. Price).

On 7th May 1993, however, the railway saw one of its most significant days: arrival of the first steam locomotive purpose-built for the railway. Named *Marri*, she attracted great interest and became the WMR's primary locomotive until withdrawn for overhaul in 2003. Another steam engine, *Nelly*, was shortly used thereafter but from 2007 the railway returned to diesel-only operation.

Marri on the turntable, New Year's Day 1994 (O. Chapman).

Trevithick in the mid-1990s (G. Fairweather).

Nikki Louise in service, 2002 (C. O'Mahoney).

Nelly heading towards the level crossing, 2006 (O. Chapman).

In April 2015 the railway was in the media spotlight when a passenger train derailed approaching the level crossing inbound, two coaches tipping over. The cause was swiftly located and rectified – a broken coach bogie spring. Although not a major accident, in an age of fast-spreading social media undreamt of when the WMR was first built, the railway received international press coverage via the media networks.

Continuing operations with a slightly simplified points arrangement for operational ease, in 2017 Jeff decided to retire from the WMR. The intention to pass the railway to a new owner had been previously raised in 2014 to long-time WMR visitor Charles O'Mahoney, Director of Southern Miniature Railways Ltd, who was looking to replace his portable line with a permanent site (emulating Charlie Reed's decision some sixty years before). In late 2016 Charles had been in discussions over another site, but difficulties with this plan coincided with an invitation from Jeff to take over the WMR. Sale of the track was agreed in March 2017, and with the Council lease arranged the railway changed hands on 29th June 2017.

End of an Era: Jeff Price's final day on the railway (A. Morgan).

The Charles O'Mahoney Years: 2017 and beyond

Now the line's fourth operator, the first service under Charles commenced on 1st July 2017. Making slight modifications to the station layout, services continued as before with both long-standing and new individuals supporting operations. On 8th April 2018 the railway reintroduced steam operation with the return of *Marri*, purchased by Southern Miniature Railways Ltd on 26th January 2018 and having her overhaul completed by Denver Light Railway Ltd. Settling into regular operations, plans are being developed to secure the long-term future of the railway and reflect its historical significance.

New Year's Day 2019, complete with Diamond Jubilee headboard (S. Mulligan).

43

Legacy

The respective owners of the WMR put much time and skill into developing the railway and ensuring its future.

Remaining down in Plymouth after he retired, Charlie Reed only once visited his former railway, many years later, when he was invited by Jeff to drive Atlantic 4442. His idea though, and the effort he put into developing all three of his railways (portable, Clissold and Cassiobury) laid the foundations of the line as it is today. George Webb strengthened the line's prospects when track needed replacing, external works reduced services, and other railways could well have been lost to history. Secured as a Park amenity, Jeff Price developed and expanded the line into a substantial and notable Watford attraction. Charles O'Mahoney, having taken on the gauntlet, has preserved its past and offers security for its future.

These individuals were and are the principle players, but just as significant is the input of many people who have made the WMR what it is today, ensuring its ongoing operation and development. More important still, perhaps, is the legacy all these individuals have left in countless childhoods, of happy days in the Park and the joys of a trip on the little railway. Long may it continue.

The Route

The railway line at Cassiobury Park has changed many time over the past sixty years, developing from small beginnings into a substantial line. Traces of its heritage can still be seen – reminders that the current route is only part of a much bigger story.

1959 – 1962

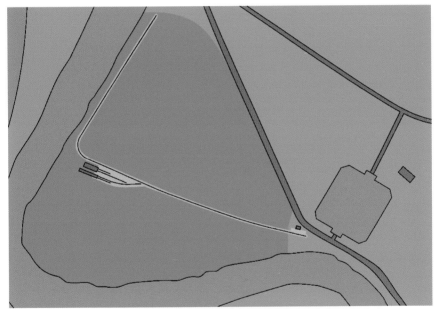

The first WMR route (Author).

Completed by the summer of 1959, the first track laid was a simple out-and-back layout roughly 150 yards long, loosely similar to his other railway in Clissold Park. Overall it formed two sides of a triangle, one side running alongside the river and the ends meeting by the main pedestrian path to the canal. At the 'station' end was a small hut that acted as a ticket office. Noted for resembling a public convenience (!) it was quickly, and more kindly, dubbed the 'Paybox'. For decoration a false 'bridge' and semaphore signal were also installed.

The 'Paybox' and initial station (C. Reed courtesy of J. Price Collection).

The line continued to a curve by the main shed before running alongside the river, trains shuttling back and forth. At this point the Council lined both sides of the river with laburnum trees. The original shed was a wooden construction built by the Council, shortly joined by an additional 30-foot metal and wooden stock shed in 1961. Built of corrugated iron into a short semi-circular structure in the style of WWII Anderson shelters, this housed the coaches and is still used today. As model-makers will know, points between tracks are costly and complex to build, so initially the railway had none – locomotives and rolling stock were man-handled across a steel plate laid on top of the rails between tracks whenever necessary and the wooden engine shed was only seldom graced by an engine once the steel shed was erected! Much of this original stretch still exists in the current line's layout.

The original wooden engine shed c.1959-60 (C. Reed courtesy of J. Price Collection).

Maid Marion on the station stretch passing the false bridge (C. Reed courtesy of J. Price Collection).

Passing by the river on the site of the original 1959 track, 2017 (S. Mulligan).

1963 – 1983

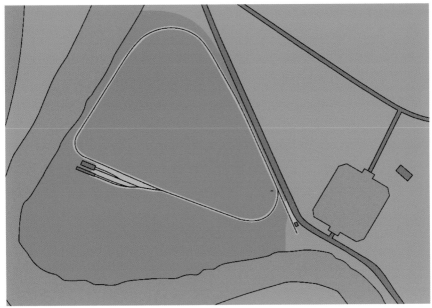

The enlarged circular route (Author).

Immediately popular, the original out-and-back layout was used for a couple of years but Charlie already had expansion in mind. As a result, by 1963 the railway had changed substantially. The original track was still in place, but now integrated into a semi-oval circuit around a third of a mile long. The 'Paybox' was rotated and formed part of a

View of the spur station (C. Reed courtesy of J. Price Collection).

dedicated station with platform, located on a spur of track separate from the main circuit near the original boarding point. The buffer end of the station doubled up as a loading bay for bringing engines in by road.

The rotated 'Paybox' and spur station (C. Reed courtesy of J. Price Collection).

Departing from the station, the train would run alongside the path until near the river. Here it curved to the left and followed the original track (as it still does today). Curving sharply again, the two sheds could be seen on the right, painted sage green. The track continued onwards before tightly curving back to the path by the station. The semaphore signal was repositioned here, mirroring mainline standards by protecting the points – the only time that the WMR has used (or needed) a mechanised signalling system. Having crossed the points, completing the circuit and re-joining the original straight, the train would perform two circuits (later one circuit) before being brought to a halt, the sprung points allowing the train to be backed down into the station to finish the journey.

Overview of the circuit c.1970s. Note the two sheds and lack of vegetation (M. Webb).

1984 – 1986

The circuit layout remained largely unchanged for decades, the railway transferring to George Webb and then to Jeff Price. It was only in the mid-1980s that the next major phase of the route's development occurred. In 1984 the overly-tight curves near the sheds and approach to the station point were re-laid. These previously had caused problems for some locomotives. A third shed was added in October 1985 and by 1986 the circuit had been fenced off.

The 1963 pathside extension, photographed in the 1990s (O. Chapman).

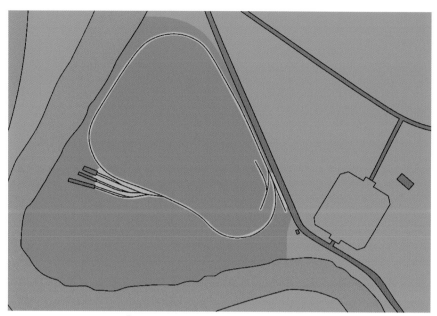

Preparations for expansion (Author).

Site of the two spur stations - first in the foreground, second beyond the metal gate (C. O'Mahoney).

More significant, however, was the station area. With the relocation of the pool in 1985 space became available on the other side of the path, triggering plans for a major extension of the railway so increasing capacity and reducing its distance from the new pool area. With permission granted it was necessary though to modify the existing station to allow these changes to be undertaken. In 1987 the entire platform was moved further up the path with the station spur and point removed in preparation for the start of extension works. Additional sidings were also temporarily laid to prepare steam locomotives and for extra rolling stock.

Passengers on the railway today may notice a stub of fencing and gate near the level crossing and, on passing alongside the main path a second shorter diamond-topped fence behind the main one. This marks the site of this second spur station's platform – the gap in the shorter fencing the original passenger entrance. This second station was though, by its very nature, to be short-lived.

The second spur station with the future level crossing site in the background. The gateway in the foreground can still be seen in the fencing today (G. Fairweather).

1987 – 1991

After these modifications in preparation for the extension project, the intended permanent changes could commence – dramatically altering the route and its overall length. The single circuit was modified into a balloon loop, adding a linking track across its centre. The 'Paybox' was finally removed; the former Park refreshment kiosk was intended to replace it as a staff area but this ultimately did not occur. In late 1988 the wooden engine shed was replaced with a larger version of the corrugated iron arch and the middle stock shed was also later extended in length. But the biggest change would occur on new ground – the opposite side of the path.

Steam-up in the 1990s (J. Price).

Trevithick approaching the level crossing (G. Fairweather).

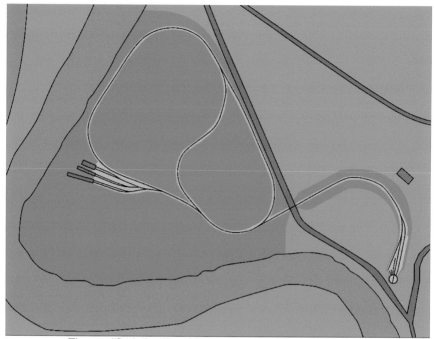

The modified circuit and temporary new terminus (Author).

Encircling the former pool site (today a grassed area with exercise machines), the line was extended some 100 yards via a manned single-track level crossing to an entirely new station by the re-positioned pools. The first terminus on this site included a

The level crossing, 2018 (S. Mulligan).

repurposed former two-foot gauge wagon turntable, with a section of redundant wheat flake factory plant as the main frame topped with a section of the C channel track from the 1950's portable railway. Unfortunately, the new terminus was accidentally a few yards out of position. While corrections were planned it was temporarily used from Christmas 1987, linked to the main track using sections of the Glastonbury Festival portable railway. The corrected station was completed by June 1991, although there was a short period when the station had two turntables!

The temporary terminus and turntable (J. Price).

1992 - 2019

The new station c.1991. Note the former temporary terminus site in the foreground (J. Price).

As built, the rectified station had two platform tracks and a single central loop track for engines to run round trains. At the far end a newly-acquired turntable was installed. This had been built for the Shillingstone Railway and was later used at the

Cornish attraction 'Age of Steam', where veteran WMR locomotive *Trevithick* had originally been built for, plus at Holsworthy before arriving at Cassiobury.

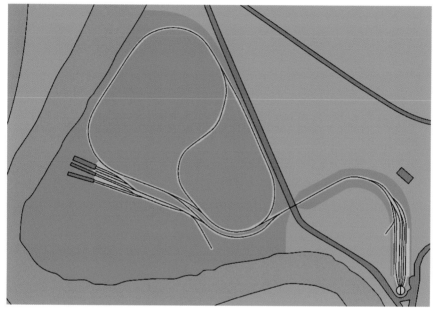

The WMR at its largest (Author).

By July 1994 there were further modification to the railway with a passing loop installed by the level crossing, a headshunt and rearranged yard layout, and the station featuring three run-round tracks, an additional bay platform and a spur for unloading engines. These led to the line's greatest overall length in its history – some 1,110 yards.

Marri in the expanded terminus station c.1994 (O. Chapman).

Nikki Louise traversing the passing loop in 2001 (above; C. O'Mahoney). Note the points connecting the running line and balloon loop, later removed (below; Author).

This layout continued in operation until 2015, when the stretch of track linking the level crossing to the balloon loop was removed. Simplifying operation, this removed four points – one of which the driver originally had to manually change each time traversed, until modified to be automatic in 1994. Along with operational inconvenience, another reason for this modification was that some passengers would occasionally try to change it as their train passed over it... Also around 2015 the single-ended track forming platform three and loading spur were also removed.

After the railway transferred to Charles O'Mahoney and Southern Miniature Railways Ltd a run-round line at the station was removed, leaving the line in the 1010-yard route currently used today.

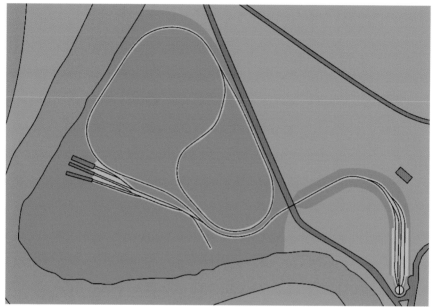

The WMR, 2019 (Author).

Modifying the station layout, 2017 (C. O'Mahoney).

Trains over the Decades

Since the line first opened there have been many locomotives working the railway. Alongside long-term residents, many fondly remembered by visitors, there have been those that only worked briefly, others in storage rarely seen by the public and visiting engines.

Originally the line operated with two engines, *Maid Marion* and a freelance shunter based on the 08 class diesels. Slowly increasing, the railway saw a height in the 1990s with eight working engines on-site, later diminishing with diesel-only operation in the 2000s. More recently, the reintroduction of *Marri* into traffic in 2018 brought the line to its current three locomotives and allows another generation to experience the sights and smells of steam at Cassiobury. No doubt there will be other engines in the future, adding to the list of historic locomotives that have been on display in the Park.

Believed to be all the motive power used in the railway's sixty year history, this chapter provides an overview of each engines known to have been part of the Watford Miniature Railway.

Marri and Chiltern Shuttle, September 2002 (D. Horton).

Jimpy

Jimpy at Rickmansworth Aquadrome, 1953 (K. Morris courtesy of J. Price Collection).

This was the first engine built by Charlie Reed and George Webb, using the acquired wheel castings that had inspired the original portable line and ultimately the WMR. Originally aiming to build a steam locomotive, the costs and materials were considered excessive, so instead they turned to a simple petrol engine in the outline of an 0-4-0 steam tank engine. Constructed in 1949 from largely recycled materials (the steam dome for example started life as a plumbers ball-cock), she was based on a scaled-up design from '*Model Engineer*' magazine and was powered by an ex-War Department single cylinder Peter Brotherhood petrol/paraffin stationary engine. The engine needed regular topping up of water coolant, resulting in the need for a trackside 'water tower' and later a tank hidden in a miniature guards van, but produced some convincing 'steam' effects!

Jimpy was first used on the portable line in 1950 and when this developed to a straight out-and-back layout she was modified with a Ford 8 gearbox to allow reverse running, also gaining spoked wheels. As the Clissold line began to be discussed it was decided that the engine needed more power, so Jimpy was rebuilt into a larger 0-6-0, later gaining a Ford 8 four cylinder car engine.

She was rebuilt again by 1958 into a 4-4-2 resembling the London, Tilbury & Southend Railway (LTSR) 79 class suburban tanks, and when the Clissold line was taken over in the early 1960s she passed to the new operators (likely with the sit-astride coaches built to go with her). *Jimpy* shortly after broke a wheel, however, and the new operators defaulted on payment. Sadly, when Charlie returned to Clissold where she had been stored he found that vandals had burnt down the shed and *Jimpy* was destroyed.

Maid Marion and Jimpy, c.1958 (C. Reed courtesy of J. Price Collection).

As far as the records are concerned, *Jimpy* never saw service at Cassiobury so cannot qualify as a former WMR locomotive. However, during research a photograph arose that could question this. In it, *Maid Marion* is double-heading unmistakably with *Jimpy* (in 4-4-2 form) on the portable track. No information survives detailing where or when, but the two engines together suggests 1958 (just before the WMR was built). The fencing and trees also suggest the location could be the upper part of Cassiobury Park where carnivals were often held. So was *Jimpy* truly the first Cassiobury engine?

Either way, *Jimpy* is important as the engine that launched three railways (portable, Clissold and Cassiobury) and led to the WMR that we know today.

Maid Marion

Maid Marion at the original WMR station (C. Reed courtesy of J. Price Collection).

An enigmatic engine complete with unusual past, *Maid Marion* was one of the first two engines to run at Cassiobury and was the first steam engine of the WMR. Her builder is unknown, some suggesting it was the famous model engineers Bassett-Lowke to a design by Henry Greenly (although unlikely) while others have suggested either private construction using Bassett-Lowke castings or even construction by the Derby Works of the London, Midland & Scottish Railway (LMS). What is known though is that she was built in the 1920s to 9¼-inch gauge, number 1070, and was based on the LMS Compound 4-4-0 locomotive design. While these prototypes had three cylinders, reusing used steam in a process known as 'compounding', *Maid Marion* was only built with two cylinders for more common 'simple' single use of steam. Her original boiler, made of riveted copper, was constructed exactly like the full-size prototype, suggesting her builder had practical railway experience, but causing great trouble with maintenance as it was difficult to dismantle!

Originally belonging to Mr R. Horsefield, district superintendent of the Great Indian Peninsula Railway (GIP), she first operated on his quarter-mile miniature railway at Jhansi, India. Known as the 'Indian Midland', this line had two stations and was used not only by Horsefield's family but also GIP staff. Working in India for twenty years, in 1947 she was purchased by the Hunstanton Pier Company, there featuring in the 1957 Ealing comedy 'Barnacle Bill' starring Alec Guinness. While unclear when, it appears it was around this time that she gained the name *Maid Marion*.

Stuck on her trailer - Maid Marion en-route from Hunstanton Pier (C. Reed courtesy of J. Price Collection).

In 1958 she was acquired by Charlie Reed for use at his Clissold Park line. The trailer carrying her broke so she had to be left overnight at the roadside, but she safely arrived at his Bushey Heath workshop where she was converted to 10¼-inch gauge. Moved to Cassiobury in 1959 she ran many of the earliest trains until the mid-1960s when she was in poor mechanical condition. Rarely used by this point, mostly just special occasions and more often acting as the station buffer-stop, she last ran on the WMR on 30th May 1966.

When the WMR was sold to George in 1968 *Maid Marion* departed with Charlie to Plymouth. Repaired and appearing on local TV she was sold to the Towans Miniature Railway in Hayle, Cornwall, before later being sold to Geoff Kichenside, latterly at the Gorse Blossom Railway in Devon. She was acquired by Jeff Price in 1994 who began a full overhaul until sold again, ultimately moving to the Ingfield Light Railway in West Sussex where she remains today.

Maid Marion departing Cassiobury again, 1994 (D. Robinson).

08 Shunter

One of the first two engines to run on the WMR, this freelance locomotive was based on the British Rail class 08 diesel shunter. Built in 1957 by Charlie Reed, the WMR's founder, it was likely a pre-emptive answer to providing sufficient motive power for operating both the WMR (proposed in late 1958) and the Clissold line.

The 08 Shunter at Clissold Park (A. Dotan).

Mechanically it was an 0-6-0 petrol-mechanical locomotive utilising a Petter single cylinder petrol/paraffin stationary engine with chain-drive to the wheels via a Ford 8 gearbox. Very much homemade, its wheels originally came off a skip! Having no space for the driver, being more akin to a scale model, it was driven from a specially adapted seat in the first carriage, leaning over the coupling to the controls.

The 08 by the WMR 'Paybox' (G. Fairweather).

66

Often referred to simply as 'The Diesel', it was initially used on the Clissold Park line, but moved to Cassiobury by 1960 after the WMR opened. When the line was sold to George Webb in 1968 this shunter became the sole engine on the line, working trains alone for the next decade. The development of the route under Jeff Price with new track and pointwork led to the shunter being retired from operation. Sold in the 1980s, it was last known to be with a member of the South Downs Light Railway around 2007, but its current whereabouts is unknown.

A view of the 08 diesel's controls and along the spur station (G. Fairweather).

The 'Terriers'

The Terrier (M. Webb).

Scale models of the 0-6-0 London, Brighton & South Coast Railway (LB&SCR) A1 class, better known as 'Terriers' due to their exhaust sounding akin to a dog's bark, one of these engines was briefly run around 1976 by George Webb. Built by model engineer Reg Day to the five-inch design of Martin Evans (suitably 'doubled up' to 10¼-inch gauge), the scale wheel flanges proved problematic on the comparatively rough track at Cassiobury, even with part beside the path specifically re-laid for the task. It was retained by George on the sale of the WMR in 1979 but was sold a few years later to a railway in Kent. Another Terrier by the same builder briefly visited to operate a separate circle of track temporarily laid for a Council event on the former pool site in 1985. They are both now privately owned at the Ingfield Light Railway.

The Terrier hauling a rare passenger service (M. Webb).

Tom Smith Railcar

The Tom Smith Railcar, 2019 (D. Matthewson).

Manufactured in 1978, this battery-electric engine was designed to resemble a British Railways diesel multiple unit (DMU) railcar. It comprised bodywork by Tom Smith and a 4-4w bogie chassis by John Locke, later being re-gauged to 10¼-inch. Jeff Price acquired it in spring 1980 along with two coaches, first using it on his portable track before occasionally being used on the Cassiobury line. Its 2-hp motor meant it had limited power though, and it was sold around 1982 to Drummond Randall for use on his railway at Biddenden, Kent. Later sold again, it currently resides privately owned in Sussex.

Meteor V

Meteor V at the spur station (G. Fairweather).

Built 1968-71 by Shepperton Metal Products, the ten members of the 'Meteor' class became well-known across Britain's miniature railways, originating from the Ian Allen organisation's 'rent-a-train'

Meteor V's Reliant Regal engine (G. Fairweather).

hireable miniature railway concept. Developed by Alistair McLeod and Alf Pitfield from an earlier 7½-inch gauge 'Thunderbolt' design, *Meteor V* (the fifth built) was constructed in 1970 and unique in being powered by a Reliant Regal 700cc engine and gearbox –

the same van make as that famously used in 'Only Fools and Horses'. A simple 2-4w-2 chain-driven petrol-mechanical design, it was built in 1970 and was trialled in Bognor Regis before moving to Hastings. Assisting with building the Prestatyn Railway in Wales around 1971-2, it went into storage (either at Hastings or at Great Cockcrow and Shepperton)

The controls of Meteor V (G. Fairweather).

before being returned to Hastings in 1974. At some point thereafter it moved again to the Great Cockcrow Railway. It arrived at Cassiobury in 1981, the first new engine on the line acquired by Jeff Price, working the line until 1996 when sold. Renovated, it has since worked multiple lines including at Waterhall Farm, Fritton Lake and Knebworth House. Today it operates at the Vanstones Woodland Railway, Codicote.

Meteor V (J. Price).

71

Tri-ang Minic

The Tri-and Minic on the portable line (J. Price).

Intended for the portable track but occasionally used on the WMR, some battery-electric Tri-ang Minic engines were acquired in the early 1980s. Built at their Canterbury works around 1963-6, they were based on the British Rail Class 71 in 'Golden Arrow' green livery, part of a short-lived attempt to provide a self-contained garden railway system. Later sold, their current whereabouts are unknown.

Atlantic 4442

No. 4442 waiting in the spur station (J. Price).

4442 at work in the Park (J. Price).

Based on the Great Northern Railway 'Atlantic' class 4-4-2 locomotives, No. 4442 was completed by Arthur Glaze in 1961 for the private railway of Colin Gilbert (one of the founding Ravenglass & Eskdale Railway preservationists) at Lapworth Hall, Warwickshire. Originally built for 9½-inch gauge, subsequently re-gauged to 10¼-inch by Severn Lamb, she later worked a line at Oakhill Manor. She was acquired by Jeff Price in 1983 from Severn Lamb, the first steam engine after *Maid Marion,* being used both on the WMR and the portable track until sold to WMR driver Martin Walker. Leaving the WMR around 2002 she was overhauled with a new boiler before working on the Ingfield Light Railway. Sold again, she moved to Berkshire in 2009.

Steam tests after rebuilding, April 1983 (J. Price).

Meteor II

The second of ten 'Meteor' locomotives built by Shepperton Metal Products, *Meteor II* was fundamentally similar to *Meteor V*. They were differences though, primarily the use of a Petter AB1 4.5BHP diesel engine with Albion gearbox and being painted red as opposed to green. Built in 1969 it operated at the short-lived Eirias Park Railway in Colwyn

Meteor II, July 2002 (C. O'Mahoney).

Bay, then lines at Hotham Park, Bognor, and Whitby, Yorkshire. Sold in 1982 it moved to Cassiobury in 1983 and had a substantial refit in 1993, including gaining air brakes. Working on the WMR until 2003, although little-used by then, it was purchased by a private owner in Gloucestershire before changing owners again, moving to Cornwall.

Chiltern Shuttle

Jeff Price driving Chiltern Shuttle (J. Price).

The creation of R.H. Morse, built in 1946 as a 9½-inch gauge rendition of an American Pennsylvania 0-6-0 tender 'switcher' (shunting engine), when completed No. 4179 featured in *Model Engineer* magazine – an example of a particularly large home-built project. As much a scale model, she featured details such as miniature steps, headlamps and prototypical sloping tender tank, alongside more essential working parts also scaled down from the prototype.

She was originally used on Morse's personal garden railway before being sold to Captain Vivian Hewitt of Anglesey (as with Flooks' *Nipper*) and, on his death, to Sir William McAlpine – one-time owner of the *Flying Scotsman*. Soon resold, she was acquired by Amersham sausage manufacturer George Brazil and thereafter by Cyril Ruff who operated her on a stretch of portable track under a new name – *Chiltern Shuttle*. She travelled across the local region until 1983, when she was purchased by Jeff Price and, after briefly working a dedicated stretch of track, re-gauged for the 10¼-inch WMR track.

Chiltern Shuttle on Ruff's portable track (J. Price Collection).

Newly acquired, Chiltern Shuttle on its temporary WMR track (J. Price).

Model Engineer magazine was correct in its prediction of the engine as 'as asset to any park or pleasure-garden railway', becoming one of the WMR's longest-standing engines. Overhauled in the early

Chiltern Shuttle, August 2002 (D. Horton).

1990s, including substantial boiler work, it was only at this point that she gained the standard WMR buffers and couplings. Working the line thereafter, it was due to the need for a second heavy overhaul that *Chiltern Shuttle* was withdrawn from traffic in 2007. Stored on the WMR after the line changed owners, she left in 2018 and shortly after was sold to David and Yvette Horton for renovation and an intended return to the WMR.

Derek

Derek as purchased (J. Price).

The Shepperton Metal Products 'Meteor' class were based on an earlier 7¼-inch gauge design known as the 'Thunderbolt'. Only two were built, completed in 1968, based on a 3hp Petter AA1 engine as a diesel-mechanical 4w arrangement. Engine No. 2 was originally used on the Beaulieu Gardens Railway, Bognor Regis, then moving to Great Cockcrow around 1981. Sold twice more, Jeff Price re-gauged it to 10¼-inch for use at Cassiobury, arriving around 1985. Remaining in his ownership, it was loaned to Paradise Wildlife Park, Broxbourne, between 1989 and 1990 where it was christened *Derek*. Returning to the WMR, shortly afterwards it departed in 1991 for the Vanstones Woodland Railway before moving to Fritton Lake, Norfolk, in 1996. Today, heavily rebuilt with little of the original locomotive left, it works on the Hastings Miniature Railway as *Jerry Lee*.

Trevithick

Trevithick, c.1991 (O. Chapman).

The WMR's fourth steam locomotive, *Trevithick* was built in 1975 by Roger Marsh for the Cornish heritage attraction 'Age of Steam'. An 0-6-2 tank engine, her fully-enclosed cab makes her particularly large for a 10¼-inch gauge engine. She ran trials on the Stapleford Park Railway, Melton Mowbray, under the name *Kingsley* in 1976, thereafter operating as *Trevithick* (named after the Cornish pioneer) in Cornwall until the attraction closed in 1984. She was acquired for the WMR on 22nd February 1987 but was in a poor condition, arriving in pieces and requiring a substantial overhauled before entering traffic for Christmas 1990. While very heavy on the track, she was a good steamer – occasionally even being fuelled on wood and cardboard. In January 1997 she left the WMR, working on the Queen Mary Hospital Railway, Carshalton, and Merton Mill Railway before moving to the Royal Victoria Railway in 2003, where she is still in operation.

Trevithick being loaded on its way to Cassiobury, 1987 (J. Nutty).

Trevithick in action. Note the standing driver (J. Price).

Conway Castle

Conway Castle newly repainted, 2018 (C. O'Mahoney).

Built by Fenlow Engineering in 1972, *Conway Castle* is a diesel-hydraulic engine with a 4w-4w wheel arrangement. One of a class of three, she and *Rhuddlan Castle* were named after Welsh castles and first operated a railway at Prestatyn, Wales, until this closed in 1979. Rolling stock and track were subsequently acquired by the founders of Rudyard Lake Steam Railway, being used there until they established a

Nikki Louise and Conway Castle – their first day at Cassiobury (J. Price).

new line in 1980 at Suffolk Wildlife Park, Kessingland. Originally operating with the two ex- Prestatyn diesels, more engines and coaches joined the Kessingland line, but in 1987 the railway was sold and most rolling stock moved to Trago Mills, Devon. Only *Conway Castle* and four ex-Prestatyn coaches remained, later joined by additional rolling stock including diesel *Nikki Louise*, working trains until the early 1990s when the wildlife park closed the railway. The remaining rolling stock and track was sold to the WMR in 1992, *Conway Castle* arriving at Cassiobury in March.

Conway Castle's first WMR train (J. Price).

While not replicating any specific prototype, *Conway Castle* was built to resemble a main line diesel engine, complete with air grills in the shape of cab 'windows'. It has only had two liveries in its time at Cassiobury – plain red (at different times being 'Midland Railway' or oxide primer in shade) and a faux main line 'Railfreight' paint scheme. A versatile and powerful locomotive, it is a firm favourite with crews – if less so in poor weather!

81

Conway Castle in the 1990s (E. Latter).

Conway Castle's first WMR livery, 2003 (C. O'Mahoney).

Conway Castle's second 'Railfreight' livery, 2017 (C. O'Mahoney).

The author driving Conway Castle in its third livery, 2018 (S. Mulligan).

Nikki Louise

Nikki Louise, 2017 (S. Mulligan).

After the Suffolk Wildlife Park at Kessingland took over operation of its railway in 1987, it was extended and additional rolling stock acquired, notably diesel-hydraulic engine *Nikki Louise*, named after the daughter of Kessingland's bank manager. An 0-6-0 locomotive, it was built in 1988 by R. Prime of Steam Powered Services specifically for the line. Unfortunately the extension had steep gradients and *Nikki Louise* was ill-suited to the task, suffering from poor performance – difficult operation generally becoming a factor behind the line's

Nikki Louise as-built, photographed at Kessingland (G. Fairweather).

84

closure around 1990. Sold to the WMR along with *Conway Castle*, coaches, and track, *Nikki Louise* also underwent a substantial rebuild, its second since construction. Coming back into regular use in 1998, the most noticeable changes to the engine were the addition of outside cranks and coupling rods, the fitting of

Partially dismantled for rebuilding, Nikki Louise at Cassiobury (G. Fairweather).

an exhaust funnel and lowering the buffers to suit WMR needs – their blanked-off higher position still visible on the engine to this day. Now loosely resembling an '04' type standard gauge shunter, *Nikki Louise* has only ever sported cherry red livery at Cassiobury, although initially it was a much brighter shade.

Nikki Louise as rebuilt, photographed in 2002 (C. O'Mahoney).

85

A drivers' eye view from Nikki Louise, 2019 (S. Mulligan).

Nikki Louise, 2002 (C. O'Mahoney).

Not a regular driver: the 'Ghost Train', 2017 (C. O'Mahoney).

In the snow, 2017 (S. Mulligan).

Marri

Marri, 2018 (S. Mulligan).

On the turntable (S. Mulligan).

Built in 1993 by Willis Light Engineering, Perth, Australia, she was the first locomotive purpose-built specifically for the WMR, and as of the line's 60th anniversary in 2019 has never worked on any other railway. A 2-6-0 weighing in at 1.5 tons, she is loosely based on locomotives designed by the Baldwin Company in America, so sporting classic 'Wild West' elements such as a cowcatcher and bell. She is unusual in Britain for her boiler – a Briggs design using a firebrick-lined firebox. More typical for British locomotives is the use of Walschaerts valve gear, while she also sports Westinghouse air brakes (as once used by the standard-gauge Caledonian Railway), complete with a working miniature steam pump.

Marri's controls (G. Fairweather).

Having been built in Australia, *Marri* was named after a species of eucalyptus tree. She was flown to Britain on 6th May 1993 in the hold of a 747 jumbo jet, touching down at Heathrow at 1:30am, 7th May. What makes this noteworthy is that she was brought to Cassiobury, prepared and steamed for the boiler inspector on the very same day! She was then modified by Northrow Engineering with buffers to match the rest of the WMR's rolling stock.

New to Cassiobury: Marri, 1993. Note the lack of buffers (J. Price).

Departing the station (S. Mulligan).

Marri diligently worked the WMR for ten years, and was withdrawn in late 2003. In 2005 she departed Cassiobury for overhaul, the very same day as *Nelly* arrived. Dismantled and spread across three sites, progress was unfortunately slow. Shortly after the WMR changed hands she was sold to Southern Miniature Railways Ltd, the railway's current owner. Completing her overhaul, she returned to Cassiobury in April 2018.

Charles O'Mahoney and Marri at speed, 2018 (S. Mulligan).

Marri on shed, 2002 (C. O'Mahoney).

Passing the river, 2018 (S. Mulligan).

A cab view from Marri (S. Mulligan).

Invicta

Invicta in the yard, April 2002 (C. O'Mahoney).

Built by Maxitrak for 7¼-inch gauge, this 4w petrol-hydraulic engine ran at Stockwood Park, Luton, until coming to Cassiobury in 1996. Re-gauged and extensively rebuilt by Northrow Engineering, it was used until 2002 when sold. Working on the Fritton Lake line, it is now privately owned in Essex.

Invicta and Chiltern Shuttle, 2002 (C. O'Mahoney).

Nelly

Nelly on the station curve (O. Chapman).

A 2-4-0 based on the Hunslet 'Alice' class narrow gauge saddle tank engine, *Nelly* was built in 1977 by Richards Engineering. First operating at Oakhill Manor, Somerset, later at the Berkeley Light Railway, she came to Cassiobury in 2005, the same day that *Marri* departed. She worked WMR trains until 2007 and left in 2014 when sold to new owners in Oxfordshire.

Nelly's controls (D. Horton).

Thomas Poole

Thomas Poole with Marri's tender, 2017 (C. O'Mahoney).

The driver's view from Thomas Poole (C. O'Mahoney).

Built in 2006 for the Poole Park Railway, Dorset, *Thomas Poole* was an 0-6-0 steam outline petrol hydrostatic locomotive constructed by Roanoke Engineering of North Devon, one of 65 such engines. Bought by Jeff Price in 2011 it was rebuilt and fitted with air brakes in 2014, working on the line coupled to steam locomotive *Marri's* tender (as a driver's seat while the latter was non-operational). Last used in February 2018, when *Marri* returned to service and collected her tender, *Thomas Poole* left the WMR later the same year.

Rolling Stock

Alongside locomotives the WMR has used a variety of rolling stock, much of it as historic as the engines themselves.

Charlie Reed Coaches

The first WMR coaches (C. Reed courtesy of J. Price Collection).

When the WMR first opened Charlie used homemade coaches built from angle-iron. These had previously been used at Clissold, being replaced there by sit-aside coaches from Charlie's portable line, and were seldom used after the first few years of the railway. For many years they sat near the sheds until scrapped by Jeff Price in 2018.

Hunstanton Coaches

The angle-iron coaches were supplemented by four articulated coaches previously on the Hunstanton Pier railway that had been acquired along with *Maid Marion*. Unfortunately incidents of vandalism to the coaches (originally stored outside chained to the tracks) caused major damage and forced some to be rebuilt. These became the

One of the Hunstanton coaches (M. Webb).

mainstay of passenger services during the 1960s and continued in operation until the early 1970s.

George Webb Coaches

Examples of George Webb's coaches (J. Clay).

These eight-to-ten seat bogie coaches were built by George in the early 1970s to replace the Hunstanton coaches after he took over the line. These were used for just over a decade until replaced early in the Jeff Price era, being subsequently used on the portable railway. They were finally withdrawn from use in the 1990s, although one saw a new existence after they were replaced in service. Essentially the same unchanged vehicle, it became a 'steam truck' – a rolling vehicle storing all the materials needed to prepare the steam locomotives for duty. It was used until around the late 2000s before being placed into storage and ultimately scrapped.

Ian Allan Coaches

In the early 1980s the George Webb coaches were supplemented then replaced by an articulated design built by Ian Allan Miniature Railway Supplies in the 1970s. Having slightly more capacity per coach than George's coaches, these were originally used on Ian Allan's network of seaside miniature railways and are still in use on the WMR today.

The first were bought in 1980 from the Kessingland line. Stored there unused, these were originally built for the Prestatyn Miniature Railway around 1972. Another set of coaches was similarly acquired

97

from a line at Whitby in 1983. When the railway was extended in the late 1980s, rising passenger numbers created a demand for more coaches. These were obtained from railways at Sandham Castle on the Isle of

The 1960s Ian Allen coach design: number K19 from Kessingland (C. O'Mahoney).

Wight, Trago Mills in Devon, and lastly the remaining Kessingland stock in 1992 when the closed railway was purchased virtually in its entirety. Since arriving at Cassiobury these coaches have all been extensively rebuilt and fitted with air brakes. By 2018 there were 18 coaches in service.

The line's coaching stock, 2018 (C. O'Mahoney).

Although the coaches may all look the same there are subtle differences with some of them. Unlike the Kessingland and Trago Mills coaches, the blue Whitby coaches are a few inches wider, have a slightly different overall construction, and are distinctive in having curved ends. The Sandham Castle coaches conversely are slightly shorter and have a painted aluminium trim fitted to their edges.

In early 2019 a further six coaches were acquired from the Hatfield House Miniature Railway. Although constructed to the Ian Allan design, these were built in 1991 by Jon Cocks and Glen Fairweather for the railway at Knebworth House. Therefore as of the line's 60th anniversary in 2019 there are 24 coaches available for service – the largest number of coaches in the railway's history.

What may be less known are the line's non-passenger stock. When the line was extended into a full circuit a grey open bogie truck was constructed by the Rainbow brothers who helped with the work. Remaining on the railway for many years, now on a private railway at Swindon, a bogie flatbed was recorded in 1993 as a display base for visiting 3½-inch gauge *Pendennis Castle*, but it left Cassiobury sometime thereafter.

The former George Webb coach 'steam truck', 2002 (C. O'Mahoney).

Re-purposed like the 'steam truck', two former bogie wagons saw service as ballast transporters (one falling over once when unevenly emptied!). These came to the WMR via a railway project at Holsworthy (previously being at Cornwall's 'Age of Steam' attraction) and originally came from the Shillingstone Railway that ultimately provided much useful material for the line. There were also several small 4w tipper wagons made with parts bought from M.E. Engineering, Finchley, which assisted with ballasting and construction of the level crossing and station extension.

Other Locomotives

In addition to the permanent fleet, several locomotives have been on the WMR as either visitors or as engines stored but not used.

Petrol Locomotive (Unnamed)

The ex-Ruislip Lido engine (M. Webb).

Never used on the WMR, this engine was purchased along with some bogies by George Webb from the Ruislip Lido Railway in 1973, the Lido line having temporarily closed. A 4w-4w Hunt petrol-electric locomotive built in the 1950s to 12-inch gauge, it was not converted to 10¼-inch gauge so was unable to be used on WMR metals. Ownership passed to Jeff Price with the railway in 1979 and it was disposed of around 1985. Heavily rebuilt, it now runs on the Shibden Park railway in Yorkshire.

Trailblazer

When George Webb worked for Pattissons of Stanmore, Managing Director Ken Hemingway became very enthusiastic about miniature railways. As a personal project in the 1970s he constructed a 4-w-4w (or 'Bo-Bo') locomotive using a Briggs and Stratton engine. Named *Trailblazer*, while still a bare chassis it was tested at Cassiobury, proving successful. Later it operated on its own portable line before moving to a Kent nursery. Today it is privately owned in Kent.

Stirling Single

Stirling Single in 1905 (J. Price Collection).

The oldest locomotive associated with the WMR, this antique engine built in around 1898 previously worked on the Pitmaston Moor Green Railway and lines at Broome, Foxhill (Farnborough) and Burnham-on-Sea. Possibly working on a park railway for a few years after the War, she found her way to a garage in Wimbledon.

Thought to have visited Watford in the early 1900s for attention to her valve gear by either Flooks and Smithies or Henry Greenly, she was built in the style of the iconic Great Northern Railway (GNR) express class, ultimately undergoing at least five rebuilds. As a piece of engineering the locomotive was truly historic. The old work on framing, motion and plate work posed as many questions as they answered: a real detective piece.

The dismantled locomotive was purchase in 1985 from Scotland; a protracted re-build being completed in 1997-8. Never run at Cassiobury, she was intended to be a prominent part of a historical display of miniature railways, but ultimately was sold in 2002, now residing on a private railway in Swindon.

The restored Stirling Single in 2008 (N. Knight).

Brightlingsea Tank

This 0-4-0 steam tank engine was purchased from Mr Hurly of Brightlingsea and stored at Cassiobury, but was never used on the WMR. Some mechanical work was undertaken before she was sold, last being recorded at work in Sussex.

The Brightlingsea engine being checked for gauge, 1980 (J. Price).

Thomas

Thomas prior to arrival on the WMR (J. Price).

Based on a 'doubled-up' 5-inch gauge 'Sweet Pea' class steam saddle tank engine, *Thomas* was built around 1984 by J. Brown and was stored at the WMR in the early 1990s. Only occasionally used, she departed for the Knebworth House line but returned in May 1993 as part of a Heywood Society event. Later she operated on the Vanstones Woodland Railway, but her current location is unknown.

The Empress

The Empress passing round the loop (J. Price).

Visiting for the 1993 Heywood Society event at Cassiobury, 1002 *The Empress* was a 4-6-2 steam tender locomotive loosely similar to the unique Great Western Railway locomotive *The Great Bear*. Built in 1933 by H.C.S. Bullock and rebuilt several times (both in visual style and gauge), her 1993 visit was her first steaming since

1962. Today she operates on the Eastleigh Lakeside Steam Railway.

Royal Scot & Pendennis Castle

Scale models of the express locomotives of the same names, these engines both attended the 1993 Heywood Society event. *Royal Scot* was placed onto WMR metals but, being incomplete, did not steam, while Pendennis Castle was displayed static on a flat truck, being constructed to 3½–inch gauge.

Ivor and Thomas

Thomas and Ivor prior to arrival at Cassiobury (J. Price).

Both purchased in November 1993 from the Skegness Miniature Railway, *Ivor* was a steam outline 4w petrol-hydraulic engine rebuilt on the chassis of a battery electric loco built by Cromar White in 1976. Its sister engine *Thomas* (previously named *Big 'Un*) was similar but was built in 1984 on a new chassis by M. Stuart. Never used in commercial service on the WMR, they were stored at Cassiobury in 1993 until sold respectively to a private owner in Hertfordshire and Delamont Country Park, Northern Ireland.

Ivor at Watford (G. Fairweather).

Fisherman and Sea Breeze

Constructed by Yorkshire Electric in 1977, these 4w-4w battery-electric locomotive also came from Skegness and were stored at Cassiobury in 1993. Unused owing to a lack of power in the Park, they were sold to private owners, with *Fisherman* ultimately becoming the only ex-WMR engine to have ultimately been scrapped.

Fisherman and Sea Breeze prior to arrival on the WMR (J. Price).

Arthur and Titan

Arthur, an 0-6-0 saddle tank from the Poole Park Railway (sold in 1997), briefly visited the WMR accompanied by *Titan*, another 0-6-0 tank engine from the Queen Mary Hospital railway, Carshalton. *Titan* was later rebuilt for television presenter Bob Symes and is now privately owned at Ingfield.

Arthur on the turntable (J. Price).

Victory

Stuart Ravell and Victory (J. Price).

The Kirby Green Light Railway locomotive Victory, built by Southern Miniature Railways and owned by Stuart Ravell, visited in early September 1993. The engine remains in action on its Lincolnshire line.

John Glenn

John Glenn, 2018 (C. O'Mahoney).

Built by Jon Cocks and Glen Fairweather (associates of the WMR) in 1994, *John Glenn* is a 4w petrol-mechanical locomotive based around a Reliant Robin car engine. It ran trials on the WMR after completion and briefly visited in 2018 from the Hatfield House Railway, covering for *Conway Castle* while under maintenance.

Pilgrim

Built in 1981 by David King Engineering for the Wells & Walsingham Railway, Norfolk, Pilgrim is an 0-6-0 tank engine. She was sold in 1986 and worked the portable 'Pilgrim Steam Railway' at steam rallies until the late 1990s when she moved to the Wensleydale Railway, Yorkshire. There she was used first at Bedale Hall in

Pilgrim prior to arrival at Cassiobury (C. O'Mahoney).

1999 and later moved to their station at Leeming Bar before being sold again in 2006 to the Knebworth House line. Found to be unsuitable for regular use there, she was only infrequently used and when the line closed in 2012 she was overhauled by the Battle of Britain Locomotive Society. On completion in 2014 she returned to Wells on loan before moving to Cassiobury in 2019.

Tales from the Tracks

Over the last sixty years of WMR operation there have been innumerable little occurrences that have brought amusement or rekindled memories of past challenges. Similarly, the line has led to fond recollections by those who have grown up with it. Turning to the individuals and stories behind the railway, here are just a brief assortment showing the less 'official' side of the railway.

On one occasion, as a jest, the railway ran its own dining service, with passengers being presented a cake and cup of tea before departing round the circuit. Previously when still a portable track, adults joining in on the fun after the children went home even had drinks on the move served by a maid…!

Occasionally there are rare mishaps. The iconic Ealing comedy 'The Titfield Thunderbolt' depicted an altercation between a steamroller and a branch line train. Cassiobury once saw its own miniature version: the ride-on lawnmower thought the train would stop; the steam engine thought the lawnmower would give way. Both were wrong!

Marri's toasted marshmallows – entertaining the staff on a wet day…! (C. O'Mahoney)

Similarly, on Bonfire Night 1994 *Chiltern Shuttle* overshot the turntable. Trains carried on running with other locomotives on each end of the set of coaches. Fortunately undamaged by her escape attempt, jacking her back onto the rails took some doing…

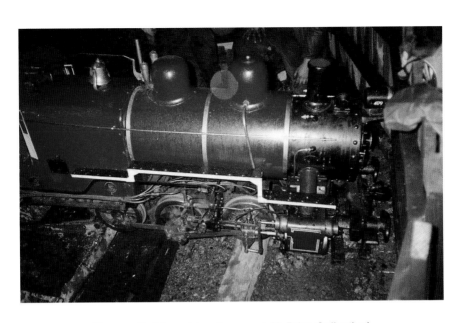

The one that (nearly) got away…! (J. Price Collection).

Such is the local regard for the WMR that it featured in the book *On Watford's Wild Side,* commemorating the rural surroundings of the town in art and poetry. (Courtesy of Myrtle Paterson & Linda Wilton)

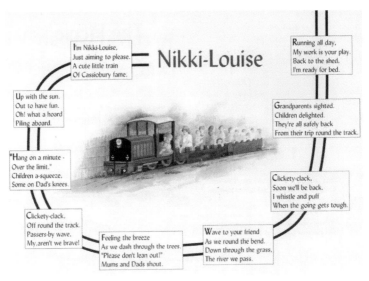

I'm Nikki-Louise,
Just aiming to please.
A cute little train
Of Cassiobury fame.

Nikki-Louise

Running all day,
My work is your play.
Back to the shed.
I'm ready for bed.

Up with the sun.
Out to have fun.
Oh! what a hoard
Piling aboard.

Grandparents sighted.
Children delighted.
They're all safely back
From their trip round the track.

"Hang on a minute -
Over the limit."
Children a-squeeze.
Some on Dad's knees.

Clickety-clack,
Soon we'll be back.
I whistle and puff
When the going gets tough.

Clickety-clack,
Off round the track.
Passers-by wave,
My, aren't we brave!

Feeling the breeze
As we dash through the trees.
"Please don't lean out!"
Mums and Dads shout.

Wave to your friend
As we round the bend.
Down through the grass,
The river we pass.

Winter 2017 (C. O'Mahoney).

Nature can often create extra challenges in running a railway, particularly for such a small rural line. While this flurry in 2017 caused wise-spread chaos on the mainline, the WMR conversely soldiered on with regular services!

Flooded: Chiltern Shuttle's last day steaming, July 2007 (D. Horton).

'Well Chiltern, I'm not going out in that.
...But Nikki - you're bigger than me!'
(D. Horton)

Over the years there have been various 'specials' run on the WMR, from parties and Park events to bonfire nights, Santa specials and ghost trains. While they take much effort to organise, the reactions of Park-users and children in particular show that it is definitely worth it. The operation of a portable track with WMR engines from the 1980s further acted as a roving ambassador for Watford and the WMR, equally supporting events in the spirit of Charlie and George's original track. Ranging from school fetes to Council events it toured the local area, in June 1986 travelling as far as the Glastonbury Music Festival...

The 'Ghost Train', 2017 (C. O'Mahoney).

Visiting Terrier and Atlantic 4442 with the portable track in Cassiobury Park, September 1986 (J. Nutty).

At the Glastonbury Music Festival, June 1986 (J. Price).

The history of the WMR is much larger than some might expect of such a railway; as shown, its sixty years have included many changes, events and individuals. Having detailed the engines, tracks and key developments, we turn to those people who have had such an impact on it. Presented in their own words, the following chapters offer the line's chronology from their perspective – their experiences and opinions. Alongside their dedication, what is particularly plain is how the WMR was more than just an occupation: it was a passion.

Thomas Poole looked out of his shed. 'It's quite wet in the Park this afternoon. I think I'll stay in the shed, nice and dry...'
(C. O'Mahoney)

Recalling the Pioneering Years

Returning to the earliest days when the WMR was little more than a dream, Charlie and George would no doubt be impressed with how far the railway has come. Malcolm Webb, son of owner George Webb and himself a former WMR driver, recalls how the line came about and began to grow.

'The origins of the Watford Miniature Railway lie in the railway interests of two men who met when they were working on the gun-tractor line at Scammell Lorries during the 2nd World War. They were C.H. 'Charlie' Reed who lived at Bushey and my late father, Watford-born George Webb (no relation to the George Webb who

owned Flanagans' funfair as we were always pointing out). Charlie conceived the idea of making money from a miniature railway but, although nothing much happened until he left Scammells to set up on his own account, I believe he started collecting useful material at that time. In those material-starved times some of the

George and Charlie (standing centre) oversee the portable track (M. Webb).

original rail was a flattened U shaped conduit used to carry the wiring on commercial vehicles. No idea where that came from but,

115

Charlie did once admit that it came in lengths that would just fit underneath the chassis of a Ford 8 hidden from view of the works' security! Some of that conduit was still in use in the sidings at Watford in my time.

I should say at this point that this was not the first miniature railway made in Watford. About 1900 two chaps formed a model engineering partnership in Leavesden Road, Watford. George Flooks was an engineer originally from Yorkshire, and Bert Smithies invented a boiler for model steam engines still used in small scale. They built a 10¼-inch gauge steam loco called *Nipper* based on a design by Henry Greenly at that time known as a writer on the *Model Engineer* magazine. One busy day in the seventies I was running at Cassiobury Park when an old chap approached and told me that *Nipper* had been built in his fathers' stable in Leavesden Road. I would have loved to have known more, but there was a trainload of punters waiting, and when I got back he had gone; I never saw him again!

In the late forties Charlie had started a small agricultural and general engineering business on Clay Hill at Bushey, known to all as 'the yard'. Initially this was side-line to his main job at Scammell Lorries. Charlie was the son of a Sheffield steel worker and had served his engineering apprenticeship at John Browns in Sheffield. He was a skilled engineer who also had a Yorkshiremans' eye for a bargain, especially with antique guns and clocks. Dad was called out of reserve to finish his National Service (in the Royal Engineers) in 1947. When he came back, he decided to join Charlie who was now working full time at the yard.

The work at the yard gave him a variety of experiences. They did everything from servicing the Bank Managers' American Cord car, to maintaining some of the fairground rides at Battersea Funfair. Customers included showmen, timber haulers (the Fensom family – famous later for their traction engines) and, in those days, there were still small farmers who wanted a cheap repair done on their binders, hay rakes etc. Most of those farms are now built over. With his army training I think that Dad was regarded as the expert welder of the outfit. One of the specialities was recon engines for the pre War Ford Y Type – the Ford 8. Dad could change one of these in less than an hour. If the engine that came out was better that the one in our Ford 8 – then that went into our car in his lunch hour! Ford 8 gearboxes figured In *Jimpy* and later in the Cassiobury Park 'diesel'.

The portable line with Jimpy and coolant water tower (M. Webb).

As Dad told it, Charlie started on the railway idea in earnest in 1950 when someone gave him some loco wheel castings to settle a debt. However I know that they been dreaming about this for some time before. The castings probably forced the decision to build and run a portable track running at fetes etc as an add-on to the business. The locomotive for the original portable railway was a scaled-up design from the *Model Engineer* magazine, an 0-4-0 tank which they named *Jimpy*. To save money although it looked like steam, it was powered by a single cylinder Peter Brotherhood (ex WD naturally) petrol/paraffin stationary engine. Dad did most of the construction and remembered having to use lots of odds and ends – the 'steam dome' for instance was made from a plumber's ball-cock! The coaching stock was of the straddle variety. To enliven things there was some 'scene dressing' including a tunnel made from a canvas

117

road-menders' shelter, There was even a scale guards van which ran on a single trailing axle. At busy times it also functioned as a popular overflow seat! It was still at the back of the shed in the Park in my time. According to Dad the original portable track was made in the form of an oval out of inch by half inch 'black iron' from the local blacksmith welded up into sections, length determined by the material available – 13 foot. Charlie once told me that he also bought a big job lot of contractors' rail from Brightmans the Builders in Hempstead Road, Watford. By coincidence my Grandma, Violet Webb, was employed there on war work during the First War and we have a photo in the family of the Brightmans girls in the yard that shows a network of those type of rails.

George Webb (left) with the portable line (M. Webb).

For the first couple of years they did the rounds of fetes and private parties. The main driver was a teenage girl Cathy who lived across the road from the yard. Eventually they graduated to straight line running which meant fitting a reverse gearbox. When there seemed a possibility of a more permanent site it was decided that *Jimpy* needed more power. It was rebuilt as an 0-6-0 with the inevitable Ford 8 four-cylinder car engine. There was some discussion over how to keep the centre of gravity low with the new power unit. Dad

118

came up with the idea of running the middle axle through a tube welded across the sump pan!

Through contacts with showmen they actually got a site at Blackpool on a fairground, not I hasten to add, the actual Pleasure Beach, but another fairground on the Golden Mile. Things went well at first but, as Bassett-Lowke found out years before, running in the sand dunes has engineering consequences not least for bearings and journals and eventually Charlie pulled the railway out before the end of the season.

Apparently, for the Coronation day in 1953 they ran at the Rickmansworth Aquadrome, and seriously considered that for a permanent site. In those days it was privately owned and they couldn't get an agreement otherwise Cassiobury Park may never have got its railway! As many have found before and since, the portable line is a lot of very hard work for little financial gain, so there were other attempts to get a permanent site. At one point they set up at a new attraction opening in Dorset, Ferndown Zoo. For some reason, the line never opened and all the tackle had to go back to the yard. At one time they came close to settling on a site in the beer garden of a huge pub on the Southend Arterial Road just next to Rayleigh Weir roundabout.

Charlie Reed on the original Cassiobury line (C. Reed courtesy of J. Price Collection).

Eventually in the early fifties, the business had to close and Dad and Charlie went their separate ways although Charlie later found a permanent site for the railway at Clissold Park,

Stoke Newington in the East End. For a time Dad and Charlie worked at the same company in different departments and as Dad recalled, they spent many dinner breaks talking railways and planning a successor for *Jimpy*. When Charlie left for another job Dad thought that his connection with the railway was over, but it wasn't quite yet...

Maid Marion and the 08 diesel on the WMR circuit (C. Reed courtesy of J. Price Collection).

In 1958 the miniature railway on the, now-vanished Hunstanton Pier in Norfolk was re-equipped. Charlie bought some of the old track and stock including the steam tender engine *Maid Marion* which was all stored in a boatyard at Kings Lynn. *Maid Marion* has always been a bit of an enigma. At one time she was thought to be built by Bassett-Lowke but nowadays it is accepted that this is unlikely. Her appearance is based on the Midland Railway/LMS three-cylinder compounds but, in fact, she is a simple two-cylinder arrangement. Over the winter of 1958 Charlie rebuilt her in his home workshop in Bushey Heath and converted her from 9½-inch to 10¼-inch gauge. He always said that the workmanship was not up to Bassett-Lowke standard. *Maid Marion* has the distinction of appearing in a British film which was actually the last Ealing Comedy made. Released In 1957, it starred Alec Guinness and was called 'Barnacle Bill', based on a story about a man who inherits a pier! I bought a VHS copy of this years ago and if you look carefully you can see that the loco was in a pretty dire state at the time.

About this time Charlie sold the Clissold Park line to a new operator with *Jimpy* as the motive power. At some time she broke a wheel and the new owner defaulted on payment. When Charlie finally went to look at the Clissold line the stock shed and stock, including *Jimpy*, had been destroyed by a fire started by the local vandals...

In 1959, using the Hunstanton stock, he built the original line in Cassiobury Park run on a concession from the Council. Charlie had retained some of the rail and later sit-in rolling stock from the portable line. The Brightmans rail and some of the conduit stuff formed the sidings, the heavier Hunstanton rail was used on the main line. Initially it was a straight up and down run with a wooden stock shed at the far end of the line. The driver was a character called Eric Sibil; he was a rather shy, taciturn, character who used to help at the yard. I was never quite sure what he did for a living but he always wore a drivers' grease-top cap with a Perkins diesel cap badge.

As in our time, the Council used to provide the tickets and take a share of the takings (NOT the profits you notice!). Tickets were sold from a small wooden shed which bore a passing resemblance to those wooden conveniences that you still see on caravan sites. We always dignified it as the 'Paybox'. This was the domain of Mrs Reed (I never knew her first name). She was a delightful person. If you didn't know, you would never have put her as Charlies' wife, they were so different. She was every inch the lady and kept everyone in order. But, bless her, she used to come up with the required 'railway cuppa' although she only drank water herself or, on very special

121

occasions, a particular brand of cider. She always referred to Charlie by his middle name: Hayden. To the rest of the world he was Charlie but never in her presence – it could be very confusing! Over the years there were numerous ticket collectors and drivers some more notable characters than others. Kids used to hang around the railway until they either got fed up and went away, or we found them a job.

The 08 diesel at Cassiobury (C. Reed courtesy of J. Price Collection).

For the first season *Maid Marion* ran the line alone, later it was joined by an 0-6-0 diesel shunter based on BR class 08. We never called it anything other than 'the diesel' although it was actually powered by a Petter single cylinder petrol/paraffin stationary engine. This was probably ex-WD and Charlie had originally built this himself for the Clissold line, by the early 1960s this did all the work. Over the years I developed a huge respect for this machine. Underneath the covers it was an ingenious arrangement with the big Petter flywheel mated to a home-made plate clutch. There was a chain drive from this to a Ford 8 gearbox. Final drive was by chain to the centre axle, all three axles joined by outside coupling rods. A clever arrangement using a sliding pillar device gave the driver a simple forward/reverse gear through a lever in the cab. The old Petter engine was originally designed to run at a constant speed .Most commercial miniature diesels used some form of fancy transmission arrangement: hydraulics, torque converters or, like Ruislip, petrol-electric. However once you learned to balance the throttle and clutch, Charlies' old diesel was easy to drive and rolled the trains over the Park line for 20 years without a clutch or engine issue that I ever heard of. It was very economical with fuel and easy to start, being fan-cooled there was no cooling system to top up. It was very much the work of an empirical engineer, but, when Jeff Price changed to the new style track and turn-outs, the long wheelbase of the diesel spelled its retirement. The wheels were actually adapted from skip truck wheels and the middle pair were flangeless. One other advantage, thanks to Charlies' eye for a bargain was that, at the back of the shed, sat a spare Petter engine and several Ford 8 gearboxes! In 20 years I know that they only replaced one gear cluster.

The 08 diesel on the circuit, 1965 (A. Horton).

Under the bonnet of the 08 diesel (J. Price).

After the railway had settled down and the pattern of the business had emerged: 'April to October, weekends and school holidays', Charlie decided on an extension to form a full circle with the station and platform on a spur. We weren't involved at the time but I know he was helped a great deal by two teenage brothers by the name of Rainbow who I think came from Radlett, as Mrs Reed would have said, they came from a 'good family'. Knowing Charlie, I suspect from his point of view that meant they did the work for fun rather than expect any substantial payment! One thing they did leave was a superbly-crafted wooden works truck which was still in use in my time.

By the time I came to drive in the mid-60s *Maid Marion* was very rarely seen, being virtually worn out. The last time she was in steam at Cassiobury Park was on Whit Monday 1966. It was one of the busiest days I ever saw, but she sat and simmered by the stopblock. She couldn't handle a train.

Malcolm Webb with Maid Marion on her last day in service, 1966 (M. Webb).

In 1967 Charlie was working as a toolmaker at an engineering firm called Gleasons on the Bypass. The American owners decided to re locate the firm to premises in Plymouth. I suspect they offered him such a good relocation package and, with retirement not far off he couldn't resist it. He offered the railway minus *Maid Marion* to my father and Dad decided to take it on. Dad ran the railway for 12 years with help from the family and a succession of young drivers. Looking back with the advantage of hindsight, I think Dad took on the railway some 20 years too late. He was in late middle-age with a demanding full time job, I was just starting a three year College course up north so I could only help run the

Travelling round the circuit (J. Clay).

railway in the holidays. It needed a bit more time and energy than Dad could give it.

Nevertheless, we kept it running and carried out a holding operation on the stock. Dad built coaches to replace the shaky ex Hunstanton stock. He devised a basic but functional bogie using self-centring bearings. We also did a lot of what is known as spot re-sleepering. The soft damp ground at that part of the park isn't kind to wood sleepers. One year, can't remember which, there was a huge drainage operation in our part of the park. We had to take up half the track circuit parallel to the river and I think we ran a reduced service. We managed to stop the contractors from doing too much damage to the existing track and Dad managed to get some useful timber for future sleepers courtesy of the site foreman.

George Webb driving in the 1970s (M. Webb).

We were lucky in that there was some engineering 'back-up', Dad worked for a small old-fashioned company who described themselves as 'turf maintenance engineers'; Pattissons of Stanmore. Nowadays they are best remembered by tractor enthusiasts for their Ford-based tractors. They built all sorts of different machines for sports grounds, built them from steel stock right up to finished article: the sort of real old-fashioned engineering that hardly happens these days. As Works Manager and later Product Development Engineer, Dad was able to use their facilities and we would have struggled without them. The Managing Director, Ken Hemingway got quite enthusiastic about miniature railways and, as a personal project, built a Bo-Bo loco using a standard Briggs and Stratton engine and reversing gearbox as used on some Pattisson Machines. In the form of a bare chassis she ran trials at Cassiobury and proved perfectly practical. Ken later built a whole portable outfit and started attending various fetes. I think he found, as did many before, that it was a bit too much to take on and sold the outfit. I understand the engine was running trains at a garden centre until recently.

Malcolm Webb at the spur station (C. Reed courtesy of J. Price Collection).

We always wanted to bring steam back to Cassiobury, we even set up a deal to buy back *Maid Marion* but the seller backed out at the last minute, a major disappointment to us. Looking back with hindsight again it probably did us a favour. The boiler was done and we would have struggled to afford a replacement. Suitable steam locos were expensive and hard to find. We did briefly run a scale model 'Brighton Terrier' in the 1970s. She was one of a pair built by a talented professional model engineer called Reg Day. She was basically a double up of a Martin Evans 5-inch design and everything was to scale including her wheel treads. She was a lovely job but the scale treads meant she wouldn't take the curves at Cassiobury. Her sister ran on a private line with proper scale track in Kent. In all conscience, she was too small for our job, but she gave us some fun and has recently been re-boilered to run on a private line.

George Webb and the short-lived 'Terrier' c.1976 (M. Webb).

This wasn't the only loco through our hands. I can't remember the details now but in the early 70s we got the opportunity to bid for the 12-inch gauge petrol-electric loco and some carriage bogies from the railway at Ruislip Lido which had been (temporarily) closed. Quite why Dad wanted the thing I don't know, but we got it cheap. One of the carriage bogies had been run with the bearings seized, the wheel was 'D' shaped! We didn't have room for the thing so it went over to

Jeff Prices' parents place, and ownership passed to him with the railway – i.e. we landed Jeff with the thing!

In all the time that Dad ran the railway I never ceased to be annoyed by the people who would come to the railway on a fine summer Sunday when the Park was crowded and say: 'you must be making a fortune!' They never knew the sheer hard work and worry of keeping it all together, the many wet days when the takings hardly covered the fuel bill or the drivers' wages and, most discouraging of all, making good the regular damage caused by vandalism.

From April to October and regularly during the winter I always knew where Dad was at the weekend – 'down the railway'. In 1979 my parents decided to move to the Isle of Wight and we sold the railway to an enthusiastic young lad who had been one of our teenage drivers - Jeff Price from Hemel Hempstead. It needed someone with energy, enthusiasm, and a business nose – Jeff was that man. Jeff has turned the railway into what it is today, long may it continue!'

Travelling on the path side stretch (M. Webb).

Onwards and Upwards

By 1979 the railway had been working for twenty years when it changed ownership, an action triggering great growth and development. Becoming the line's longest-working operator, Jeff Price describes the changes and improvements he undertook that would transform the WMR and make it the railway recognisable today.

Jeff Price and the 08 diesel (M. Webb).

Before the beginning....

'There was a railway and steam connection in my family: my paternal grandfather was a railway ganger working for the London & North Western Railway then the LMS in the Watford area. My maternal grandfather was a steam roller driver in Wiltshire, then Buckinghamshire after which he ran a public works business in

Hemel Hempstead. A youngster I was surrounded by things mechanical and steam. My first steam railway recollection is seeing a tender locomotive running across the Marlows viaduct in Hemel Hempstead at the age of about three – steam engines in the sky – impressive. I was keen on metal work and engineering drawing at school and on leaving became an engineer apprentice for a 4 year term

Early exposure to WMR

Originally I was a customer on the railway during family visits to Cassiobury Park in earlier summers and had heard about it being extended at a family Christmas gathering in Watford. This would have been the track being laid alongside the footpath to make a complete circle in the winter/spring of 1963/64.

Jeff continually improved the trackwork, such as widening the tight pathside curve in the 1980s (J. Price).

My first involvement with the operation of the miniature railway in Cassiobury Park was in the summer of 1969. This came about as a result of a cycling trip along the Grand Union canal and a visit to the miniature railway site to find George and

Malcolm Webb re-sleepering track near the loco sheds following a visitation by Thames water and resultant track damage. George Webb had taken over the previous summer from Charlie Reed so

such track work instead of operation was unhelpful. The upshot of the visit was that I started to help as a ticket collector and dogsbody.

Within a couple of years, I was made up to driver and then 'person in charge' (PIC). This carried on until the mid-1970's when having a small car made long distance adventures at weekends possible, I then carried on as a backstop driver.

Jeff Price driving the 08 in the 1970s (M. Webb).

George had decided to retire to the Isle of Wight in the spring of 1978; adverts for the sale of the WMR were placed but no buyer was found who would keep the railway on site at Cassiobury.

Railway ownership

During the Easter Holidays in 1979, while visiting Cassiobury, George Webb suggested that I might consider taking on the WMR and offered easy terms to enable the deal. Thus from 1st May 1979 I was the owner/operator of the Watford Miniature Railway: one locomotive, three coaches, a circuit of track, a couple of spare bogies and the sheds. Watford Borough Council caught up with events and first a licence, then a ten-year lease were arranged to regularize the situation.

My first purchase was a Battery Electric DMU built in the early 1970's, a couple of venerable Parvers bogie coaches from the 1930's and a steel point from Atherstone. A nice steam locomotive ex-Poole park was beyond my means. The issue with having a Battery Electric DMU was that it had to be taken home in my van to be recharged! Another early purchase was an 0-4-0T steam engine from Brightlingsea built by a Mr Hurly, very cute but never steamed.

High winds or vandalism? Meteor V discovering a bin on the line, September 1990 (J. Price).

The first useful acquisitions were the five ex-Ian Allan coaches from the Prestatyn miniature railway via Brian Nicholson at Kessingland and the petrol locomotive *Meteor V* direct from Ian Allan Ltd, collected from the Great Cockcrow Railway. We were now on a roll: two working locomotives, more coaches that could be fitted in the sheds and some less useful items of rolling stock to add to the mix. Membership of the miniature railway enthusiasts group, The Heywood Society was gained in 1980; this provided an introduction to the UK miniature railway scene and long standing connections have resulted.

While all this was going on, good fortune smiled on the WMR and support was offered by A.C. Fincken, Imperial Way, Watford – manufacturers of Force wheat flakes. Their principle shareholders were the Fincken family, who were also miniature railway enthusiasts. Thus a small workshop was created across the road from the flake production plant and some storage of excess equipment was possible. It is through their good offices that a batch of new 12lbs/yard ASCE steel rail was purchased from Luxembourg to enable the railway to be re-laid using only about four different rail sections rather than the hotchpotch of rail sections up to then.

Jeff Price and 4442 in the 1980s (J. Price Collection).

Changes to the layout

Very early on my watch, consideration was given to making a more interesting route for the railway, some plans being presented to WBC. The reaction was mixed, the newspaper cuttings of the time tell the tale clear enough. Nothing happened.

The old padding pool build in the 1930's was causing concerns – this brought the creation of the new paddling pools, the new toilets and kiosk together with the plan to relocate the playground .This went on for a couple of years; the end result was the old paddling pool was filled in and the railway planned an extension to move the station area closer to the playground.

During this process, there was support from WBC officers but as the newspaper reports of the time show, support from others was mixed. The people of Watford are

Chiltern Shuttle at the extension terminus, October 1996 (E. Latter).

in the debt of Councillor John Watts who supported a miniature railway and park for the people of Watford. Councillor Watts was Mayor of Watford for 1989 to 1990.

The Wrong Tree

View across the station site, 2000. Note platform three and the loading spur to the right (C. O'Mahoney).

The WMR extension plans were approved, a lease created and work started, however, it became apparent that a clear misunderstanding had arisen. Construction had started of both the railway and the new path/playground but it was clear that both were trying to occupy the same slice of land!

A meeting was called on site: it emerged that the railway planning application, based on WBC maps, had revolved round the wrong tree on the map. The result was a narrowed pathway between the river and paddling pools, the submission of an additional planning application for extra space, a revised lease and the narrow platform next to the path. Hindsight!!!

Meteor V running round a train c.1994-6 (J. Price).

People involved with WMR development from 1979

The WMR had been helped with legal work with WBC by Peter King, a then-recently retired solicitor, local resident and wildlife supporter; he introduced his son Nick King and Tony Prior who both helped in other matters. Peter was a great supporter of the wildlife in Cassiobury Park, as had his father.

Peter introduced Vic Ashwell, another local retired resident who helped with track building, fence erecting and tending the crossing gate for many years. Vic had been a 'guest' of the Japanese following the fall of Singapore – such things he and others endured. Vic had a very clear view of what was right, talked of events before the War in a detached manner, the fall of Singapore and his work in Africa after

Trevithick in the loop (G. Fairweather).

the War. Tales from a distant past. He was strong on engineering training and a supporter of the friends and wildlife groups based in Cassiobury Park.

Percy Robson was another early helper, a banker by trade, was able to provide some basic business guidance. In the early 1980's The Donkey Man appeared. A man of few words, who seems to have been of another age altogether, he said he had been a wheelwright from the days of horse drawn vehicles. He had at some point had an accident with a chain saw, luckily he gained a large scar and retained his leg. He plodded up and down the pathways with his two donkeys, occasionally defending his occupation from 'modern thinking people'. It would not be allowed now...

Helen and Juliet Quaterman plus Sue Belbin all provided support in their Sixth Form and university years. Juliet had the distinction of splitting a set of points with the first train of the day due to a stone being jammed in the blades (by persons unknown) holding them open. On my arrival I found several people standing around the derailed locomotive (*Meteor II*) on the grass in the vee of a set of point completely clear of the rails!

Contact had been maintained with Ruislip Lido Miniature Railway society since it took over the Lido railway in 1979. A member there, Brian Boreham, was very keep to help at Watford to drive the steam locomotives. His help provided a link to Dennis Howells who owned GWR pannier 9466. I was able to help support Dennis and his locomotive for ten years in the 1990's which included the amazing London Underground Ltd. (LUL) 'Steam on the Met' operation each May for two weekends that ran into Watford Metropolitan station. The WMR ran out of coal one weekend and Brian was able to 'borrow' some LUL coal from the locomotive at Watford Met! This connection with main line steam resulted in a long standing involvement with myself and some WMR staff members that is ongoing today. A good education in the greater rail industry for those involved.

Chiltern Shuttle and Marri, 2003 (D. Horton).

Brian was chatting with me over lunch one summer's day between trains, on a bright June weekday. He related his brief war time career as a Major in the Commandos. It comprised of 'we landed on a beach, the chap next to me fell face forward, dead. We found some German's in a bunker shell shocked, the back of my calf was shot off, I was evacuated off the beach, woke up in hospital in England and later married my nurse.' All very matter of fact. It was some years later after Brian had died that it became apparent that the beach landing was in fact the Dieppe Raid in 1942. Brian was mindful of his luck and he supported young people unable to lead 'normal' lives in a quiet but practical way.

Nikki Louise (prior to rebuilding) and Trevithick, 1992 (J. Price).

In the early 1990's contact was made with Northrow Engineering in St Albans. Run by John Cousins in part of the PPH Coaches depot, John rebuilt and overhauled most of the WMR locomotives and rolling stock. The fitting of air brakes, anti-lock oval buffers, wheel turning, locomotive re-engineering (*Conway Castle, Nikki Louise* and

138

Meteor II), overhaul (*Chiltern Shuttle*) and running repairs (loose fly crank on *Marri*, loose crank pin on *Trevithick*). John was also able to master keeping steam driven air pumps supplied with spare parts etc. He was a very accomplished model engineer of the old school and was awarded a Model Engineering Exhibition Silver Medal for a 7¼-inch gauge BR Standard Class Five. Full of practical engineering solutions and experience, he has left a legacy of some fine model and work. How fortunate the WMR was!

Heavy work: jacking up Marri for running repairs (J. Price).

The Walker family had a long involvement: Martin was helping in the early 1980's, his children Ian and Max then Julie all helped for long stretches over the years. Martin introduced Tony Johnson and his son Andrew. Andrew had a life changing experience when he suggested to a passenger that there was no need to get hysterical over some matter. The passenger promptly DID get hysterical. Andrew disengaged in a rather shocked state saying *'I am never going to tell someone not to get hysterical again'*. I am sure the experience is helpful in his career as an airline pilot!

Another long term visitor and supporter of the WMR has been David Robinson. He has been on site with his camera at key moments in WMR history – the fact that he provides dates on his prints has helped provide the WMR's timeline.

One of the upshots of membership of The Heywood Society was connections in the wider miniature railway community. A very significant contact for the WMR was meeting Joe Powell of Ashton Keynes, Wiltshire. He had a splendid 10¼-inch garden railway and his own

Topping up water, 2003 (D. Horton).

engineering business. He was able to undertake wheel and axle machining for the WMR bogies together with some tricky work on some of the WMR steam locomotives. Also in his barns around his engineering works storage of some WMR equipment was undertaken. An engineer of the old school, he would 'walk round a job' before starting. He and his workshop are no longer with us, however, his workmanship will be around for a long time.

Two-train operation in the 1990s (E. Latter).

Another great resource for WMR was Derek Holsworth who whilst working at Renegade Engineering then Harbour Jig and Tools, both Watford based engineering companies. If we broke it, he would weld it; body panels for locomotives pressed, folded, engineered. A resource that was well used over the years. We delivered the problems, Derek delivered solutions.

Other WMR staff and helpers of more recent years have been covered in Dave Horton's recollections below. However, I would like to record the help and assistance that Vince Marsala and extended family provided over the year while he ran the ice cream van, kiosk and paddle pools.

What has changed over the years: 1979 to 2017

1979
Saturday was a shopping day, Sunday was the day out with the family. The general physical size of the population was light or medium build. Passengers belonging to ethnic minority groups were the exception. Most people were not particularly concerned with what their dog left where. Glass bottles and cans were the main drinks containers. The grass was cut short over most of the park. WBC employed a direct labour workforce for most activities. The public walked into the park from home, public transport or cars parked outside the park. It was not uncommon to see people of a certain age with severe facial burns – maybe one of the few from the summer of 1940...

2017
Sunday is a normal shopping day, passengers more evenly spread over the weekend. Passengers are from a diverse ethnic mix and I would hope people are more tolerant now than in 1979. Thoughtless dog owners are now the exception. Plastic rubbish is in the ascendancy. Grass mowing is restricted, the wildlife have a ball. Most WBC work is contracted out. The size of a car park defines the success or otherwise of a leisure venue; very much a restriction on the use of Cassiobury Park by the masses. People of a certain young age are seen living with limb loss in the recent service to their country. Mobile phones with cameras will record anything people wish: social media means this can be shared across the world with ease. However, the unrestrained (and un-moderated) comments left by some on a local paper's website following the spectacular derailment in April 2015 were shameful. So much for progress.

The Public

Without the public there would be no Watford Miniature Railway. The public are a random mixture of people in a public park with no filter of an admission fee. The result is that many people were a joy to meet and talk with to understand their thoughts and experiences. One such was Tony Putman, a local model engineer, retired from Rolls Royce. His contribution to the railway was being talked into making the foundry patterns for the cast signs that have provided guidance to passengers and the cost of the ride for many years past.

The fares signs, 2002
(C. O'Mahoney).

4442 at the 1983 Watford Carnival (J. Price).

However, during the warmer months there are some whose disruptive presence is unfair on the many. If only they would ask of themselves what they expect to achieve by their actions... It is not the children's fault: look to the parents. Other people are just difficult for whatever reason.

Towards the end of my time in Cassiobury Park, a trend started of a grandparent telling me that when they were young they would ride on the train with their parents, they in turn took their children on the railway and now they are taking their grandchildren on the railway. The comment 'you were the driver then!' – I think it is time to retire.

The Rainbow Brothers' wagon with Maid Marion (C. Reed courtesy of J. Price Collection).

Progress 1979 to 2017

I started with lots of enthusiasm, for a number of years up to the mid 1990's the support from Council officers had been good and objective. There had been a Head of Leisure supported by departmental mangers who had been in post for a number of years and therefore knew the ropes within WBC.

The station extension, New Years Day 1994 (O. Chapman).

When the 1997 lease renewal was undertaken, the above situation had degraded to no Head of Leisure or department head in post. The result was our point of contact at WBC was a junior manager who had no interest in the matter at hand nor the prospect of any development of the offering that the WMR could provide. At that time, a number of historic 10¼-inch gauge scale steam locomotive had been acquired with the concept of constructing a display building with modern-world staff facilities to back onto the station area. This idea was completely ignored, the WBC officer only had time to deal with a lease renewal on a like-for-like basis as he had a considerable workload already.

The lease was renewed, I considered my options, which were putting my energies into expanding the WMR against the apparent indifference of the WBC leisure department or develop the other business that I was involved in. The latter course was taken, with the collection of scale and historic steam locomotives being dispersed. The WMR carried on as a successful miniature railway but with limited horizons.

Extreme flooding - July 2007 (D. Horton).

The railway has survived floods, (many) falling trees, some vandalism and the odd item in the river over the years. Santa specials have been run for charitable groups, operation on the firework nights for the Round Table have been interesting. Since that time, the WBC Leisure department has been repopulated, the Hub development is the result. However, it is sad that the opportunity was not taken to enhance the railway as part of that project.

It became clear during the lease negations in 2016/17 that the terms that were offered were not going to be attractive to me thus in March 2017 I advised WBC that I would not be seeking a renewal.

Jeff Price's last day on the WMR, 2017 (A. Morgan).

It is Watford's good fortune that Charles was able take over in July 2017 so the WMR has a dynamic new owner with enthusiasm and vision. I hope that the efforts of those who have gone before will be capitalised on by WBC in supporting Charles as he moves forward.

I am very grateful for the long term support of Angela Price, my sons Oliver and James plus Sue Jonas who have all helped to keep the show on the rails. For anyone who has been left out in the forgoing, I am sorry for the omission, however, I am sure that everyone involved over the years wishes Watford Miniature Railway a bright future, continuing the tradition that a visit to Cassiobury Park is not complete without a ride on the miniature train.

Passing on the legacy of 'Come on Dad, let's have a ride on the train...' for the people of Watford.'

More Than Just A Railway

The WMR is special for most of those who have travelled and worked on it over the years, but driver David Horton probably has more to owe the railway than most. In his own words, he recounts his experience of the line's more recent history.

'My first memories of the Watford Miniature Railway were as a very young boy. My paternal grandparents lived in Cassiobury Drive, and most Sunday afternoons were spent there along with my sister and parents. To illustrate what a long-established institution it is, my father and his siblings used to ride the train when they were children too.

The Horton Family on the railway, 1965 (A. Horton).

When I was a kid, after lunch or before 'tea' we would often go down to the Park, weather permitting, it also being an opportunity for my late grandfather to walk his dog Tessa. A ride on the train, as well as going to look at the canal boats, was mandatory.

These early memories, in the late 1980s and early 1990s, are somewhat hazy. I remember the line when it was just a circle of track, the old station being adjacent to what is now the level crossing. The locos I can picture are the Meteor diesels. I don't recall any steam in those early years although *Chiltern Shuttle, Trevithick* and the Atlantic must have arrived on the scene about that time. The ride was two complete circuits. I recall that '*Thomas*' flags were sold at one point, and this was very exciting!

Chiltern Shuttle, 2002 (D. Horton).

When I was around ten I was deemed responsible enough to volunteer as a 'young supporter' at the nearby 12-inch gauge Ruislip Lido Railway. Exhilarating at first, the line was in the throes of completing their first steam locomotive, *Mad Bess*, and extending the line by about a mile. I couldn't wait to get started on cleaning the engines and helping with the trackwork. Alas, it was not to be, for after about four months I was called upon to dress up as an elf for their Santa Specials. Being a fairly self-conscious sort of boy, I declined and, suitably disillusioned, jacked in the whole thing!

Luckily my mother, who has the gift of persuasion, must have recognised how disappointed I was, so had a quiet word with WMR owner Jeff Price. We were told that there was a 'bit of a waiting list', but in the late summer of 1995 I was invited to start volunteering at Cassiobury Park. My first day, donning second-hand overalls which were far too big for me, I was given a bucket of paraffin and a brush and introduced to the motionwork of *Trevithick*. I meticulously cleaned this all day, apart from spending some time opening and closing the crossing gates. When I came home that evening I 'reeked of paraffin' but I was in seventh heaven. My railway career had begun.

Trevithick ready to depart (G. Fairweather).

Trevithick was a locomotive of slightly odd proportions, as many miniature steam engines are. Looking more like a proper industrial locomotive than a miniature engine, it had Joy valve gear and overhung the rails quite alarmingly – such that anybody driving it had to either stand carefully in the middle of the cab with their head sticking out of the 'sunroof' or, if there were two people on the footplate, they had to make sure they were carefully balanced on either side. The loco was in a bit of a sorry state and didn't really go

149

'chuff' for all that I remember – more of a 'woof'. It left the WMR in 1997 and is now at the Royal Victoria Railway, near Southampton.

I gradually obtained more and more responsibility throughout my teenage years, learning at first the basics such as taking the fares, operating the turntable, coupling and uncoupling, manning the crossing gates, opening up and putting things away each day. Opening and closing the shed doors had a special technique all of its own – a combination of skill and brute force. Another important 'training point' was crowd management on busy days, and how to tread that fine line

Trevithick running round her train (O. Chapman).

between assertiveness and rudeness when dealing with difficult punters.

Marri and Chiltern Shuttle double-heading services, 2003 (D. Horton).

As all of us youngsters soon found out, Jeff had a particular way of doing everything. We didn't always understand the full nuances of why, but woe betide we tried to do it differently or fell into lackadaisical ways and you'd never hear the end of it! As maturity set in, it became obvious why things were the way they were; most of it was either down to safety, security or operating efficiency. Jeff had run the railway for many years before I came along, quite often single-handedly, and like any self-made businessman it was normally the case that he had learned to do things in certain ways through bitter experience.

Leaving the station (D. Horton).

In those early days I worked with a good variety of people, some of whom we still exchange Christmas cards with. There was Tony Johnson and his son Andrew (the latter was later to become an airline pilot). Martin Walker and his sons Ian and Max, and later his daughter Julie too. Ian and Helen Woolward, who emigrated to Tasmania, they were great fun to be around and Ian had some wonderful stories of adventure. Colin Jeffrey, who went on to a career in the rail industry, like me. For a few years there was an older chap called David Robinson. Then there was dear old Vic who came down at the weekend to help on the gates – he had been a war veteran and was quite a character. My best friend at the railway was Phil Morton, who was very close in age, started working there just before me, and was a fellow railway enthusiast at heart. Phil very

151

much 'took me under his wing' and not only did we spend many happy days playing (for it was playing, to us) with *Marri*, *Chiltern Shuttle* and *Trevithick*, but we also spent hours round each other's houses attending to Mamod steam engines and oo gauge model railways.

At school I was simultaneously teased for being a 'trainspotter' but also slightly admired (perhaps) for having a pretty cool job which allowed me to work outside in beautiful surroundings, doing a variety of practical tasks, interacting with the public, and most of all getting paid to do something I enjoyed. It was far better than the average paper round anyway and I got a nice 'tan' on my arms in the summer, or was that oil and coal dust? Who knows! I often saw friends and acquaintances from school at the weekends when they came down to the Park with their families and I suppose the offer of a free ride helped to temper the teasing, which I'm glad to say never turned into bullying.

Two in steam, September 2002 (D. Horton).

Preparations on-shed (D. Horton).

Things started to get more interesting around 2000 when I entered sixth form and somehow around six of my friends ended up getting a job at Cassiobury too. I forget what order they came in but there was Chris Cardwell, Steve Bunting, Ben and Matt Higginson, Pete Keltie and Pippa Kingston. Joining the ranks were some slightly younger folk too – Scott Littledike, Kayleigh Curtis, Katherine Ellis, Richard Callaghan, Hannah Maguire and Ben Dimmock. It truly was a sea of young faces. I think Jeff took some quiet pride in this. Not only was he giving us what was, in retrospect, a rather unique start in our working lives, but in return he got the benefit of new ideas and energy.

Ready to start (D. Horton).

153

What made life slightly difficult for the 'roster clerks' (quite often me) was that six of us all played in a Big Band together, and as that became a success in 2001-02 we found there were some periods with virtually nobody available to run the railway.

In November 2001 a young lady named Yvette Phillipps started with us. The daughter of an engineer, and very much into model aircraft and model railways, she didn't say much at first but soon showed a flair for getting things done and making the whole operation run like clockwork. It wasn't quite love at first sight, for various reasons, but in 2003 I asked her out and the

Waiting for the turntable (D. Horton).

rest is history – we are now married with two children. Yvette often reminds me that during those years when I was away doing stuff with the Big Band, she got a pay rise because of being practically the only person left behind to run the railway. In return I often remind her of the famous incident involving *Marri* and the lawnmower!

The years 2000-2003 really represent the highlight of my time at the WMR. Old enough to run the place ourselves, my friends and I had virtually free rein. This allowed Jeff to focus more time on running his other business. We took pride in operating things at Watford as efficiently as possible during the high days. The best times (and also the most exhausting) were those hot summer days when it was 'one in one out' with the heavy, fully-loaded trains departing alternately from platforms 1 and 2. Occasionally, if we had enough suitably competent steam drivers, we would run a two train, *entirely steam* service using both *Marri* and *Chiltern Shuttle*. In the evenings we would quite often retire to the 'Swan' in Leavesden, talk for hours, get home after midnight, then come back and do it all again the next day. Great fun, great times.

A ride on the footplate – Charles O'Mahoney and David Horton (E. Latter).

It is worth mentioning at this point a young lad called Charles who used to visit every so often with his grandparents. Carrying his trademark 'Fisher Price' camera (as we rather unfairly and derogatorily called it), he was always a quiet one but seemed to take it all in and show an interest. Before long we were letting him go down to the shed to explore and take photos, we would give him 'footplate rides' on *Marri* and even let him drive and fire under supervision. Then he'd disappear for several months on end and we'd think nothing of it. One day, up popped a website by Charles, featuring 'interviews with the engines', which gave us a chuckle. Anyway, little did we know. More of that later...

Soon everybody in my age group was departing for university and the beginning of 'real life'. The younger ones dutifully carried on until their time came to move on as well, but seemed less inclined towards steam, so the use of *Marri* and *Chiltern Shuttle* sort of fizzled out. Perhaps we older ones were guilty of having had too much of a good thing, and had failed to pass on some of the skills. Anyway, 2003 was the last year in which I spent anything like a significant amount of time at the railway, after that it was only the occasional weekend until I graduated in 2007.

In April 2003 we had both *Marri* and *Chiltern Shuttle* operating together for what, we think, must have been the last time. To commemorate this great event, one day we connected all available carriages together and did a 'double header', along with some other silly antics – perhaps the less said about this the better.

On the move: double-heading from the driver's perspective (D. Horton).

Nelly raising steam (D. Horton).

Around 2005 a new steam locomotive appeared, albeit briefly – *Nelly*, modelled on a Quarry Hunslet. Although it was efficient and very easy to operate, it somehow didn't have the character of *Marri* and *Chiltern Shuttle*. It was too easy! But worse, it was somewhat prone to a bouncy ride and derailed rather too often for its own good.

156

In July 2007, with the locomotive wheezing and gasping on its last legs, I steamed my all-time favourite engine, *Chiltern Shuttle*, for the last time before her boiler ticket expired and she was literally 'sent to the back of the shed' (to paraphrase the Rev. Awdry's books). On this day there was virtually nobody in the Park because the heavens opened, and by mid to late afternoon a lot of the railway had flooded. I eventually accepted that there was no point in carrying on, put the loco away, the fire went out, and that was that. I will always remember that day: to me it was rather poignant as it represented the end of an era.

Amid the floods: Chiltern Shuttle's last day in steam, 2007 (D. Horton).

Fast forward a decade, a lot has changed in our lives but Yvette and I can still count several of those people from the halcyon years of 2000-2003 as close friends, including Jeff and his family – long-suffering wife Angela and the 'Half Prices' James and Ollie. In 2009, Yvette and I married and Phil was our best man. Not many years later, along came two children, Florence and Daniel, who are both now well into the process of being 'indoctrinated' with railway enthusiasm.

Due to the realities of me wanting to work in the rail industry, we moved away from Watford to Derbyshire, then to Somerset, but continue to visit the WMR on a fairly regular basis thanks to parents (now grandparents) still living in the area, as well as most of our friendship group. Every visit to the WMR we are welcomed as 'old hands', even the newer people we never worked with seem to know us well. Never missing an opportunity to 'have a drive', our children struggle with the concept that not everybody's parents are allowed to just rock up and drive the train. We are grateful that Jeff and his staff continued to allow us such a privilege. We always said that it would be a sad day when we turn up at the WMR and nobody knows us!

In 2017, ownership of the railway passed from Jeff to Charles O'Mahoney – you remember that kid I mentioned earlier? Well it turns out that he grew up and did an Engineering degree, started his own business, and ended up taking over the WMR. Mad fool! We were delighted that somebody like Charles took on the baton. A guy with a passion for the railway at heart, he has got some great ideas about how he wants to develop things – the future is in good hands.

Letting off steam (D. Horton).

In early 2018 Charles shocked us all by announcing that he'd purchased *Marri* and that, after an absence of a decade during which it had been given a major overhaul, it would be returning to steam at the Park in a few short weeks. Having duly 'landed' at Cassiobury on 3rd April, it didn't take Yvette and me long to fall prey to the enticing photos and videos and roster ourselves (as volunteers) to spend a day rekindling the magic with *Marri*.

In late 2018 we returned the shock treatment by purchasing *Chiltern Shuttle*. She had always been the more challenging locomotive to drive and fire when compared to *Marri*, and as such, when you got it right, you

Starting the overhaul, 2019 (A. Walton).

really felt like you had conquered something. Built in the early 1940s by R H Morse of Woodmancote, West Sussex, she is a fascinating little locomotive with a tale to tell – and to my mind as close as one can get to the 'real thing' in miniature. Handled carefully, she can pull a fully-loaded ten-coach train with ease, thanks to her big cylinders and all the weight on three coupled axles. For generations, loco men and women have developed emotional attachments to particular locomotives and this is definitely the case with *Chiltern*. I had been saying for years to my friends that one day I wanted to buy her. They said I was mad. But now she's finally ours – that particular item on the 'bucket list' ticked off. It will take several years and quite a lot of money to restore *Chiltern Shuttle* but she'll be back at Watford, no doubt, delighting and inspiring another generation of children and young people and yes, unashamedly allowing us to wallow in nostalgia too.

David Horton at the controls of Nelly (O. Chapman).

To sum up. As it says in the title, the WMR has been to me, to Yvette, and many others, very much more than just a railway. It was an integral part of both my childhood, and my formative years. Thanks to Jeff, we started our working life on a sure footing, learning many life skills along the way. Thanks to Jeff, I was introduced to 'big steam' too – the heritage railway movement. Thanks to the WMR, relationships have been formed that will last for a lifetime. Quite frankly, it has a lot to answer for – my happy marriage and two children being chief amongst that. And as those children grow up, we hope they too will come to hold a special place in their hearts for the WMR.

Here's to the next sixty years!'

How It Happened For Me...

Over its history the WMR has been supported by many individuals, from the staff keeping the trains running to the passengers who have enjoyed the results. For some though, the railway would have a bigger impact that one would expect, as the line's current owner, Charles O'Mahoney, explains...

'Life has a strange circularity to it.

When I was a little boy no trip to see my grandparents in Watford was complete without a visit to Cassiobury Park. Officially this was to walk their dog, Gretchen the miniature schnauzer, but of course there was always time for a ride on the miniature railway; my first ever train ride was at Cassiobury as a babe in arms. When I was five or six I would daydream that one day I might be able to drive the train in the park, as lots of children do.

Charles O'Mahoney and his brother with Conway Castle (E. Latter).

As I grew older, I got to know the railway's owner Jeff Price and some of his staff, and at one point even set up a rudimentary website for the railway. Visits to the Park would now often mean the chance to ride on the engine with the driver, or to look at some of the spare engines hidden away in the shed. At the

Charles O'Mahoney with driver Max Walker and Conway Castle (E. Latter).

age of 13, however, my family decamped to the West Country en masse; visits to Cassiobury now became infrequent, though I would often pop in for a quick look when in the area.

Marri, 2000 (C. O'Mahoney).

Lots of people have a trainset when they are a child but grow out of it as they get older. In my case, as I grew up the trainsets gradually got bigger, from the OO gauge trainset on the table to a model steam railway out in the garden, then to a miniature railway running up the side of one of our horse fields! Once you have a miniature railway you find it is a small world, and every so often my path would cross that of Jeff Price. I would normally ask how the railway at Watford was, and eventually Jeff gave the impression he would like to sell it if the right person came along. At the time I thought nothing much of it...

'Playing trains' probably wasn't a sensible career option so I went off to university to study Mechanical Engineering. After graduating a plan to take some time to work out my best career move turned, only slightly by accident, into running a business which (amongst other things) undertook engineering work for miniature railways. When a portable miniature railway came onto the market locally we bought it, and spent a few summers touring it around country shows and vintage rallies. Operating a touring railway is hard work (as Charlie Reed had found); after a long day's running you then have to pack the railway up completely and take it away. So, I started keeping an eye out for a suitable site to have a permanent railway open to the public. In a roundabout way this culminated with me receiving a phone call from Jeff Price in March 2017:

The 'other' portable line (C. O'Mahoney).

'I'd like to talk to you about Watford. I've decided not to take a new site lease from the Council. Are you interested?'

Here was the railway of my childhood being offered to me on a plate. The only snag: I lived 250 miles away and didn't have all the money required. Ultimately, however, the only answer could be yes, although I suspect my family and friends thought I was mad for doing it (but they were all too kind to say!).

Of course, taking over the railway meant not only did I have to negotiate to buy it from Jeff, but also negotiate a new lease for the site with Watford Borough Council. Fortunately, both negotiations proceeded smoothly over the next few months; I should thank here David Bass from the Council who handled the negotiations for them. Everyone involved was keen to secure the future of the railway and made things as easy as possible.

One of Charles' first train as owner, 2017 (S. Mulligan).

At the end of June 2017 Jeff gave me the keys and, for better or worse, I was now in charge. My first day of operating was 1st July, a very sunny Saturday with the new Hub building and refurbished paddling pools opening to the public for the first time. Although some staff had come with the railway, none were available to help on day one – and so on his first day of retirement Jeff kindly offered to come down the Park and help drive trains! In fact, Jeff has always been quick to offer support and advice when needed; regulars will be pleased to know he still maintains an interest in how things are going and pops in for a visit occasionally.

The first summer was a steep learning curve as I came to learn the vagaries and quirks of running the railway. The inherited troops of Amy, Kieran, Michael, Ollie, Stephen and Rick were soon joined by Simon and Estere, who had both turned up in the Park asking for jobs. Ben, who had first started on the railway back in the early 2000s, helped out a few days as well. However as the staff were still a little thin on the ground I only had four days off all summer, and that was only because it poured with rain on those days.

Before and after: the 2017 tree fall (C. O'Mahoney).

There were the odd challenges that summer too. One Sunday we turned up to find a large tree fallen right across the track by the crossing. I had brief visions that we would be unable to run trains for days whilst we arranged for the tree to be removed. Fortunately, I managed to find someone able to cut it up and move it, so we were running trains again that day by 2pm. Another day, one member of staff managed to derail an engine whilst putting everything back in the sheds, and it was at that exact moment the skies chose to open in a downpour. The August bank holiday Monday had two trains running around in the sunshine packed to the rafters all afternoon, but only three of us working – it was so busy that poor Stephen got stuck on the crossing gates for four

'Oops!' (C. O'Mahoney).

hours, as each time he looked up there was another full train already heading towards him.

After the first summer in charge I was quite pleased to shut the shed doors on a Sunday in September and have a week off! With the number of passengers tailing off as we moved into winter, we needed less staff each day, so I managed to get that rarity of odd weekends off as well. If I'm not in the Park the staff are broadly trusted to keep the show running and only call me if they really need to. There are two types of phone call I get from the staff on a day off:

1. *'This has broken, we can't fix it, but don't worry we've still got a train running.'* (This normally happens when I'm at least 200 miles away so can't help anyway.)

2. *'It's freezing cold, we've had two people all morning; there aren't even any hardy dog walkers in the Park – can we pack up and go home?'* (The answer is of course yes.)

The Summer of 2017 (S. Mulligan).

By Christmas of year one I had a feel for how the railway was running and realised it had been more popular than I anticipated. The railway had run with only diesel locomotives for the past decade, but it had always been my intention to bring a steam locomotive back to the railway – and it looked like it would now be possible, much sooner than I thought. Jeff still owned two of the

166

railway's old steam engines, *Chiltern Shuttle* and *Marri*. *Chiltern Shuttle* was in one piece but in need of a thorough overhaul to get her running again. *Marri* was dismantled in many parts scattered across three different locations, however, most of the overhaul work needed had been done; '*she just needs putting back together*'. By the time I had crunched numbers and come to an agreement with Jeff it was January, but I viewed *Marri* as

Chiltern Shuttle, 2014 (C. O'Mahoney).

a late Christmas present. In order to get her up and running as quick as possible whilst I was running the railway, I shipped all the parts up to an engineering company in the Midlands, Denver Light Railway, and told the company's owner Andy Walton to get on with putting her back together.

Marri coming together again (C. O'Mahoney).

Rebuilding Marri (C. O'Mahoney above, A. Walton below).

Finished! (A. Walton)

Marri was back in steam by March 2018, and on the 3rd April Andy delivered her back to the park with his 4x4 and trailer. Unfortunately, here we hit a problem. The site of the railway absorbs rainwater like a sponge, the spring weather had been quite damp, and the unloading ramp round at the station (which drains very well as the drain for the old paddling pool is still buried under there) had been removed many years ago. We have an access track to our sheds which is built on rubble and well made up ground, but this ends just before the sheds. We did the best we could to tow Marri in, but ultimately ended up with the 4x4 stuck up to its footboards in the mud, with the trailer hanging over the mainline at a right

Back on track (C. O'Mahoney).

Steaming up again (C. O'Mahoney).

angle. Somehow – I am still not entirely sure how – with little more than a handful of willing people, a few planks of wood and some shovels we got the car out, rotated the trailer and unloaded Marri. The only suitable thing to do now was light a fire and give her a test run. By late afternoon steam was raised and I took Marri round to the station. No one had been told that she would be back that day, and when she arrived on the turntable the playground emptied completely with everyone coming to have a look. Steam was back and it looked like it would be very popular.

First train after overhaul, 2018 (C. O'Mahoney).

Marri's big test was the first bank holiday weekend in May. The sun shone, people just kept appearing, the paddling pools and playground were a sea of children, and many of our fellow businesses and organisations in the Park had never seen it so busy. Fortunately, *Marri* rose to the task admirably, putting in a six-hour shift where she was ready to go every ten minutes as required. A new member of staff also had the misfortune to start on that day as well! As I said to him '*If you can cope with today you can cope with any day here*'. On the Tuesday after I suspect we all had a very good lie in.

Resting in the sun (S. Mulligan).

The second season started seeing a procession of old staff showing their faces; word had got out that things were happening on the railway and the old hands wanted to come back and see. Top of the list were Dave and Yvette Horton, who couldn't resist coming back to drive steam trains occasionally. Chris, who had left a few years before I took over, decided coming back on the staff for a few days a month was a nice way to spend his weekends. In August we had an evening gathering of around twenty staff old and new; with some food and drink to hand, we spent the evening playing trains and catching up until it got dark. Many staff have spent their formative teenage years working on the railway and one or two came up to me that evening to say: *'I hope you're enjoying it, this was the best job I ever had!'*

In early 2019 I had a phone call from Stuart Madgin, who ran a railway at Hatfield House just a few miles away. He had been given unexpected notice to leave and needed to clear the site – a shock for everyone. The little railway community is a friendly one and we all help each other

Double-decker trains: shunting the Hatfield coaches (S. Mulligan).

out, so I mobilised our team and spent a few days helping Stuart dismantle his railway. The upshot of this all, however, was quite unexpectedly I ended up with some more track, coaches and sheds for Watford! The track had originally been supplied by my predecessor Jeff, so in a strange sense it was all coming home. With extra track in stock I think an extension to the railway will now be on the horizon, but we will have to wait and see what exactly happens.

Since taking the railway over I have become aware just how much the railway means to the residents of Watford. It's a bit of a cultural institution – not a day goes by where we don't have someone who rode the railway as a child return with their own children, grandchildren or even great-grandchildren. I hope that it will continue for many more years to come; we are working to develop plans to really secure the railway's future and reflect its historic significance as one of the oldest park railways in the country.

Cassiobury gets a bit bleak on a cold Saturday in January when the rain is blowing sideways, and there are odd 'challenging' day where something plays up and tests your patience. However, the Park is a beautiful place to work and we bring joy to thousands of people each year. The other day I was asked to estimate how many people had ridden the railway, and after a few minutes scribbling on the bank of an envelope concluded we have probably had the best part of three million passengers over the last sixty years.

Things were brought home to me one day recently when a young boy boarded the train with his grandparents and their dog – which was a miniature schnauzer. As I went along the train collecting the fares, the grandfather said to me:

'We always have to come on the train with our grandson, he'd love to drive it when he's older.'

My reaction? Well...

'You probably won't believe this, but when I was little I came on the train with my grandparents and their schnauzer. I always wanted to drive the train then, and now look what I do!'

The WMR Fleet, January 2019 (S. Mulligan).

173

Those Who Made It Happen

With thanks to the following who have worked on the railway over the years and helped to make it the success it is today. Our apologies to those we may have inadvertently missed out.

Michael Albon
Vic Ashwell
James Baldwin
Sue Belbin
Brian Boreham
Steve Bunting
Richard Callaghan
Joe Carter
Cathy (surname not recorded)
Chris Cardwell
Keith Chesworth
John Cousins
Kayleigh Curtis
Ben Dimmock
Daniel Dowling
Kieran Duke
Katherine Ellis
Brian & Christopher Fincken
Bob Ford
Ian Gabriel
Anthony Gould
Richard Gregerson
Ken Hemingway
Ben & Matt Higginson
David & Yvette Horton
Colin Jeffrey
Tony & Andrew Johnson
Sue, Chris & Amy Jonas
Pete Keltie
Peter & Nick King
Pippa Kingston

Scott Littledike
Adam MacDonald
Hannah Maguire
Vince Marsala and extended family
Ken Morris
Philip Morton
Simon Mulligan
Rudi Newman
Charles O'Mahoney
Joe Powell
Jeff, Angela, James & Oliver Price
Tony Prior
Tony Putman
Helen and Juliet Quaterman
The Rainbow brothers
Chris Rayment
Charlie & Amy Reed
David Robinson
Percy Robson
David Saunders
Eric Sibil
Stephen Stacey
George Storrow
Estere Tamma
Martin, Ian, Max & Julie Walker
John Watts
George & Malcolm Webb
Ian and Helen Woolward

Acknowledgements

With grateful thanks for the assistance of:

Philip Devonport
Amir Dotan
Daniel Dowling
Vicky D'Souza
David Henshaw
David Horton
Simon Mulligan

Charles O'Mahoney
Jeff Price
Oliver Price
Chris Rayment
Peter Scott
George Storrow
Malcolm Webb

Everyone who has provided information, images and stories.

Some of those who made it happen, August 2018 (D. Horton).

End of a long day (S. Mulligan).

Picture References

Owen Chapman
Jennie Clay
Amir Dotan
Daniel Dowling
Glen Fairweather
Anne Horton
David Horton
Neville Knight
Eric Latter
David Matthewson

Alan Morgan
Simon Mulligan
Rudi Newman
James Nutty
Charles O'Mahoney
Andy Walton
Myrtle Paterson & Linda Wilton
Jeff Price
Malcolm Webb